FLORIDA: THE WAR YEARS 1938-1945

By
Joseph & Anne
Freitus

FLORIDA:
THE WAR YEARS
1938-1945
By
Joseph & Anne Freitus

First Edition
First Printing

ISBN: 1-891118-30-7

Published by
Wind Canyon Publishing, Inc.
P.O. Box 1445
Niceville, FL 32588-1445

Editor: George Jaquith
Layout/Design: Becky Jaquith
Cover Design: Wind Canyon Publishing, Inc. ©1998
Back cover photos courtesy of Aviation Heritage
Other photo credits are noted by each photo.

Dedication

In memory of Captain Colin Kelly, Jr., a Congressional Medal of Honor recipient from Madison, Florida who lost his life on an air mission near Midway Island during World War II.

Acknowledgments

We are enormously grateful to many individuals who contributed writings, recollections, advice, time and material. These include:

Melanie Odom, Reference Librarian, and all the patient staff of the Venice Public Library, we thank you for your time and tolerance. We also thank David J. Coles of the Florida State Archives for his advice and direction; Carl Creel, a volunteer at the Fort Myers Historical Museum; Ron Williamson, Chief Historian for NAS Jacksonville; Dr. Abraham Scherr of MacDill AFB; R.M. Browning, Jr., Historian of the United States Coast Guard; Taryn Rodriguez-botte, Director of the St. Augustine Historical Society; S. Platt, 2nd Lt. USMC, Public Affairs Officer at NAS Pensacola; Bernard F. Cavalcante, Head Operational Archives Branch, U.S. Navy; Robert P. Widner of St. Petersburg; Dwight V. Blevins, AT2, Public Affairs Office at NAS Key West.

Also we express our deep appreciation to Lt. Col. Norman L. Redding, Headquarters of the Florida National Guard at Camp Blanding; to Howard Melton of the Arcadia Historical Society; and to Betty Arnall, Director, Historical Resources, Venice.

We express special appreciation to Anne Webb, AFHRA at Maxwell AFB for spending so much time in sorting through records and files.

We also thank the many local historical societies for their gracious help and continued assistance. Our requests were many, and their kindness always offered.

A special note of gratitude is extended to our editor, George Jaquith, for his commitment that this account should be published, and his patience, and to Becky Jaquith for her skills in working with some difficult photographs and in laying out the book.

[And if I may be allowed some lattitude in praising my companion, wife, best friend and co-author, Anne, for her life-long help and encouragement. J.F.]

About the Authors

Joseph and Anne Freitus are freelance writers who have authored three previous books:

160 Edible Plants of Northeastern U.S.
Wild Preserves
The Natural World Cookbook

Their interest and research into wartime Florida have covered many years, both from the perspective of being long-time Floridians and because the more they learned, the more they realized that the achievements in Florida during the war years, 1938-1945, were not widely recognized. Mr. Freitus served in the Navy during the Korean War. Mrs. Freitus recently retired from a career with the United States Postal Service. Both are involved in volunteer organizations and activities.

Introduction

Florida: The War Years 1938-1945 is an attempt to focus the attention of our younger generations on the significant contributions made by an earlier generation. A generation of youth confronted with the totality of a world at war. A war so total in its scope, commitment and destruction that it was beyond anything previously experienced by man. Unlike past wars, World War II was a terrible experience shared by Americans from all walks of life, race, gender and economic backgrounds. All worked and sacrificed together in a common cause to defeat the powerful forces of militarism that sought to dominate the entire world.

Floridians united against the forces of evil by turning their state into an industrial arsenal for war material and a vast network of airfields to be used for the training of American and Allied pilots. Millions of citizens played their part to see that the foundation for the best training possible became a reality. Many were to give their precious lives in the process. The reported deaths of pilots and aircrews within the 1938-1945 aviation training programs numbered, unofficially, 27,000. Florida realized 1,092 deaths with the loss of 941 aircraft.

Many individuals who experienced Florida during the war years will protest the omission of some detail they feel strongly about; however, the inclusion of such fine detail would yield a book too ponderous to enjoy. We present a brief accounting of several different topics.

World War II proved to be the most important event in Florida's long and rich history. Therefore, it deserves to be long remembered.

Now a few words about the names of bases. For the most part we have used the names in use during the war years. In some instances the authority for a base has switched from one branch of the military to another. In some instances a base was called by two names. In some instances simple error created an incorrect name. Consider the following examples. Homestead was Homestead Army Airfield during the war years and is Homestead Air Force Base now. Ditto with Eglin. Venice was always Venice Army Airfield, but the painter-preparer of the sign at the gatehouse (as shown on page 29) incorrectly called it Venice Army Air Base, a name which was then used interchangeably with Venice AAF. Please bear with us in these designations. In every instance in the book, there is a reason why the name in use as cited is used.

Finally, an explanation of the photographs. Almost all of the photographs used in the book are old and rare. Many were not allowed out of the archives in which they are housed. [For good reason — one shipment of our own photographs to our publisher never arrived and still has not been located by the shipper.] In those instances we photographed the photograph because we felt the content was particularly useful in the book. In the case of very old photographs, they were not taken and stored with the thought of later appearing in a book, and so, many of these do not have the clarity of professionally shot and stored photographs. Nonetheless, each has a place in the book because it helps tell a remarkable story.

Joseph & Anne Freitus

CONTENTS

CONTENTS

Chapter One

The Approach of War

Tourists, as well as Floridians, were about to close out the year 1939 on a note of optimism and a growing faith in the national and local economies. The dark days of the devastating depression were fast disappearing as the changing economic situation reached deep into Florida.

Ignored by most Americans, a second World War was about to explode onto the world stage. With legislation that declared their neutrality, the average American little dreamed that one day thousands of their young people would be fighting and dying in far-off lands with strange sounding names.

World War II began at exactly 0431 hours, September 1, 1939, when three sleek German dive bombers (Ju-87s) burst from the lowering overcast and destroyed two major railroad bridges spanning the Vistula River, near the city of Dirschau, Poland, northwest of Warsaw.

Two agonizing days later Poland's allies, Great Britain and France, declared war on Germany. Poland's outmoded air force was destroyed on the ground before it could offer any suitable retaliation. Within thirty days the German and Russian Armies had overrun all resistance. During the struggle, Great Britain and France, bound by a mutual aid treaty, attempted to rescue Poland from the onslaught of the German war machine, whereas the United States adhered to its policy of neutrality. A sizable portion of the population remained neutral through 1941 until Japan attacked Pearl Harbor. Most Americans believed that the onrush of the war was not America's war. It was a war that involved Europe and the Far East with Japan and China. Neutrality was not only a word and an idea but it was a protective shield as well as a potential economic boom.

While voices like Charles A. Lindbergh warned that Americans should not become entangled in a European war, there were others who cautioned that it would be impossible for the United States to remain neutral. They foresaw the most devastating conflict the world would ever know and, in its maddening fury, would involve the United States. Prepare for the inevitable was their watchword.

Legislators in Florida heard the message and were preparing for what seemed to be a worrisome future. Voters in 1940 elected as Governor a World War I veteran from Bartow, Florida — Spessard Holland. Serving as a county judge from Polk County and as a State Senator, Holland's wartime administration was noted for solving many of the State's long standing financial problems. Prosperity was slower in returning to Florida compared to its neighboring states. The war years would only serve to postpone many of the problems related to the economy.

With the 1939 invasion of Poland by Germany and Russia, the American military realized the shift in air tactics. The blitzkrieg, combining massive air power with fast moving armored units, achieved spectacular victories. Prevalence of the neutrality mentality initially slowed development of all branches of the armed forces, especially the Army Air Force, resulting in an initally ineffectual air arm.

Beginning in 1938 various agencies of the Federal Government and the military devised ways of paying lip service to the restrictions of the Neutrality Act while still preparing for war. In addition to increasing the size of the armed forces and armaments, Congress passed the Civilian Pilot Training (CPT) program. It provided free aviation training to qualified college students.

In addition to pilots, planes and more troops, the United States needed training bases, qualified instructors and suitable locations for bases. Army flight training was centered at Randolph Field in San Antonio, Texas, producing 500 pilots per year. Navy flight training, located at Pensacola on the Florida Panhandle, increased its training facilities in order to train more pilots.

General of the Army Air Force, Hap Arnold, watched as the Army increased its bases and inductees. He realized to build another facility such as Randolph Field and train 500 pilots a year would take anywhere from five to six years. This was not a suitable means of building an air arm required to fight a global war.

Calling together a small group of World War I and a few civilian flyers, they quietly devised a plan to train more military pilots. Utilizing their own private, commercial-flying schools, they planned to radically overhaul the flight training program. The system worked so well that by 1944 the United States was producing 110,000 pilots each year.

Commercial flight schools in Florida geared up to meet the expected demand. There were Greenville Aviation School at Ocala and Lodwick schools at Avon Park and Lakeland. Dorr Field and Carlstrom Field were located at Arcadia with Riddle-McKay Aero School at Clewiston. The U.S. Army Air Corps quickly sent cadets to these commercial flying schools.

Located in northwestern Florida at Pensacola Bay, NAS Pensacola has served as the seat of Navy air training since World War I. Five nations have flown flags over Pensacola, beginning with the early Spanish, French, English, Confederates and the United States. In 1826 the United States constructed a Navy yard south of the city to serve its ships in Gulf waters.

World War I established Pensacola in 1917 as the Navy's flying school, training pilots for such aircraft as fighter planes, balloons and dirigibles. In 1926 Corry field was added, increasing the size and capability of NAS Pensacola. With the increase in tensions between Japan and Germany, Pensacola increased its operations, adding a flight instructors school, a school of aviation medicine, aviation maintenance and aerial gunnery. With the increased emphasis by the Navy on carrier warfare, Pensacola was ideally situated. It offered flight training and the difficult carrier takeoff and landings. The development of this technique was to prove a turning point in the war, especially in the Pacific.

Intense lobbying by the Jacksonville Chamber of Commerce persuaded Congress to sign into law on April 26, 1939 a bill authorizing the aviation facility at Jacksonville. A $1.1 million dollar bond issue was voted by the citizens of Jacksonville and Duval counties. In July 1939 the land at Black Point on the west side of the St. Johns River was purchased and given to the Navy for a naval air station.

During the Army Air Corps maneuvers in 1938, pilots had been impressed with the flat sandy snake-infested stretch of coastal land near Tampa known as "Catfish Point." At this time far from town, noise from the aircraft would not be a bother to the local citizens.

In January 1939, a Federal Commission screened locations for six new airfields, one of which would be located in the southwestern United States. After much wrangling, the Mayor's Commission, composed of Tampa's leading citizens, was able to convince the Federal Commission to build the new Army air base at Tampa. The new base was named for Col. Leslie MacDill, a World War I pilot who died in a plane crash near Washington, DC in 1938.

The site was purchased by the Hillsborough County Commission at a cost of $97,000 and donated to the Federal Government. Tampa then leased Drew Field to the Army for 25 years at $1.00 per year. Three airfields actually existed in Tampa during the war. MacDill, Drew Field (the present site of Tampa International Airport) and Henderson Field, present site of the Busch Gardens. MacDill became the headquarters of Army's Third Air Force Command.

With the threat of war, Governor Holland reactivated the State Defense Council which Governor Catts had instituted during World War I. With the backing of the State Legislature and the Defense Council, Senator Claude Pepper lobbied Congress for Florida's share of the increasing war production. The W.P.A. increased road building, especially those associated with defense installations. By the end of the war the State Road Department was maintaining about 8,000 miles of highway in Florida.

Senator Pepper was able to convince Congress and the various branches of the military of the great areas of flat, unoccupied land and the state's greater than average number of flying hours, its excellent weather and the fine rail service that Florida was noted for. The East Coast was served by track all the way from Jacksonville to Key West, and crossing the state to Tampa south to Fort Meyers. The availability of the rail network meant the Armed Forces would be able to move vast amounts of war material with little trouble. Several good harbors such as Tampa, Jacksonville, Miami and Fort Meyers were available to handle large seagoing cargo ships. Instead of developing Texas as the primary military training facility, this role was shared with Florida.

The increase in various defense activities was felt in Florida long before the country became involved in the shooting war. Thousands of service men and women from the United States and Allied countries were sent to the new bases to staff them and serve as training cadres.

War finally broke upon the people of the United States on December 7, 1941, changing Florida forever. In 1941 Governor Holland activated the Florida National Guard. 3,841 Floridians were immediately assimilated into the Army as the 31st "Dixie" Division. During the war, 254,000 men and women from Florida served in various branches of the armed forces.

The Florida Defense Council, headquartered in Tallahassee, activated its 137 local and county councils. Activities ranged from emergency firemen, policemen, medical teams, air raid wardens, aircraft warning systems, motorcycle patrols and enforcement of blackout regulations.

With the bombing of Pearl Harbor, Congress, no longer impeded with the burden of the Neutrality Act, hurriedly enacted a program known as the Development of Landings Areas for National Defense (DLA). The Civil Aviation Agency (CAA), with the cooperation of the military, selected sites that would be considered for national defense and training. Many local governments anticipated this development, purchased land and offered it to the CAA for possible training facilities.

Senator Pepper, with other influential Floridians and local business groups, quickly persuaded the CAA of the many benefits of locating military bases, especially airfields, in Florida. Many airports already existed in Florida and these communities were eager to offer them to the military. With CAA funds, barracks, hangars, sewage treatment facilities, housing, administration and other buildings were rapidly added. Local contractors employed increasing numbers of workers in their rush to meet the demand of the needed military bases. Florida was in a hurry everywhere.

The Army was more aggressive in its airfield construction, responding to the many offers of land. Competition soon developed between the two branches of the military, each bidding for the same sites. Early in 1942, the "Stratmeyer-Towers Conference" established a policy which divided Florida down the center of the state. The Army would develop its airfields on the western half and the Navy on the eastern half. This arrangement satisfied both branches, as it did not include existing facilities, such as Jacksonville, Pensacola, MacDill and Key West. The Army later violated the agreement by building Morrison Air Base at Palm Beach.

Despite some violations of the accord, cooperation between the services was considered good. Depending on how one differentiates between a primary or auxiliary airfield, before the end of the war 227 airfields and other military bases had been constructed throughout Florida (whereas there were six military bases in Florida in 1941). Many of the airfields returned to the public domain, enlarged to become updated jetports.

One of the largest Army training facilities was constructed near Starke in northcentral Florida. Not only did Camp Blanding process and train thousands of inductees, it also contained and processed prisoners of war. Altogether the POW base at Blanding administrated more than 4,000 German and Italian prisoners, scattered throughout 15 branch camps.

Tourists facilities were quickly converted to meet the wartime needs of the military. Hotels, inns and houses were utilized to house officers and enlisted men. By the first year of the war, the Army was using 70,000 hotel rooms located at Miami Beach. In addition to housing personnel, many hotels served as training centers, schools, officer candidate schools, and restaurants often became mess halls. Some branches of the military quickly utilized tourist hotels throughout Florida, thereby saving the need to build similar facilities. Many college campuses became training facilities involving upwards of 10,000 men and women. A WAAC training center utilized Daytona Beach; a Naval training center used the Hollywood Beach Hotel; the Ponce de Leon at St. Augustine became a Coast Guard center; and a Navy gunnery school was located at the famous Hotel Fritz in Miami.

Few Florida industries, including agribusiness, went untouched by the war. Before the war commenced, the cattle and citrus growers were already supplying ever-increasing tonnage to aid war-torn England. Cotton, tobacco, sugar, corn and other crops were suddenly in great demand. With the need for munitions, Florida's phosphate mines increased output, working around the clock. Expectedly, the need for skilled workers, engineers, administrators and many other related occupations increased. With the wartime emergency and increasing need for men and women in uniform, women began to assume traditional male jobs. America quickly discovered that men and women handled the milling machine, turret lathe or welding rod with equal skill. "Rosie the Riveter" may have been a song popularized during the war, but it served to express the new role of women. Women in the present day workplace owe much to their wartime predecessors.

Black Floridians and other minorities did not find the same degree of success as white workers. Segregation persisted even in war-related industries, yet even this offered an economic alternative to the staggering poverty in depression pre-war Florida. Most American minorities were generally restricted to menial, non-skilled jobs. Those black Americans who joined the Armed Forces found themselves still segregated, restricted to all black units commanded by white officers. There were many notable exceptions such as the famous Tuskegee Airmen, but generally minorities were forced to serve in units that were confined to menial labor. After the war, all this would begin to change.

Tourism and real estate were dramatically affected by the blackout regulations, a fear of German submarines along the coasts, coastal patrols, civil defense and the OPA with its rationing of gasoline, butter, meat and cooking oils. All this served to restrict tourism. A lack of hotel rooms also served to decrease tourism. The influx of over 1,000,000 servicemen and thousands of foreign trainees replaced the tourist dollar with the G.I. dollar. No increase in the number of military bases, servicemen and women, nor the change in the workforce, could account for the reaction that served to change Florida. Four years of war only served as a catalyst for change that triggered a series of chain reactions and events that continue today. The history of Florida during the war years from 1938 to 1945 is written in names — names of the many airfields, bases and the people who have returned to live in the Sunshine State. Mention to a pilot who trained in Florida, or a WAC or WAVE that served here, and a conversation will follow of names and places that will never die or be forgotten as long as people remember World War II and all that took place.

Chapter Two

Camp Blanding

The present day Camp Blanding owes its remarkable history and location to the Florida National Guard and the U.S. Navy. The Navy in 1939 wanted to establish a Navy air station on land bordering the St. Johns River near Jacksonville. The site, however, was the location and training facility of the Florida National Guard, known as Camp Foster. In mid-1939, a land swap was negotiated and a 30,000-acre site was selected in Clay County as a National Guard camp and so began the history of Camp Blanding.

What follows is the genesis of Camp Blanding as written by Brigadier General Ralph W. Cooper, Jr. (Retired). This written history is provided by LTC. Norman L. Redding, Training Site Manager, Camp Blanding.

In the early days of the Florida National Guard, training was more or less a haphazard affair with field training being conducted at various available locations. During the 1905 session of the Florida Legislature, the matter of a permanent campground for the Florida National Guard was considered and a commission was appointed to locate a site for the training of Florida National Guard troops.

At the 1907 session of the legislature, the commission presented their recommendation for a site at Black Point, about 15 miles south of Jacksonville on the west bank of the St. Johns River. The recommendation was approved, but no appropriation was made for the purchase of the property.

A group of citizens in Jacksonville raised between $6,000 and $7,000 and purchased the site, consisting of 300 acres, and deeded it to the Armory Board (which consisted of the Governor, the Adjutant General, the State Quartermaster, and major commanders). Thus came into being the first site for the permanent training of Florida troops.

The Secretary of War, recognizing the need for a rifle range purchased an additional 400 acres to the north and contiguous to the state lands and a rifle range was constructed. For a number of years field training of troops, not only from Florida but also from other southern states, was conducted at Black Point. Facilities were meager and housing consisted of tentage.

Then came World War I and the National Guard was mobilized. The Government established a cantonment at Black Point and named it Camp Joseph E. Johnson. Wooden barracks, mess halls, latrines warehouses, administration buildings and hospital facilities were constructed. Many troops were trained here prior to embarkation for Europe and the site took on a semblance of permanence.

Subsequent to World War I, the camp was returned to the Armory Board and again became a training area for National Guard troops from several southern states. The facilities that were left proved a great asset and Camp Johnson was used effectively for training.

On June 18, 1928 Major General Clifford R.

Foster, the Adjutant General of Florida, died in office and Brigadier General Vivian Collins was appointed to succeed him. A short time later the Armory Board changed the name of Camp Johnson to Camp Clifford R. Foster.

During the late 1930s, with war brewing in Europe, the United States began giving more attention to military preparedness. The Navy desired to acquire Camp Foster and convert it to a Navy air training station. The Secretary of War approved the conversion and provided the sum of $400,000. Salvage rights of existing facilities were made available to the Armory Board to establish a new training facility for National Guard troops.

The citizens of Jacksonville, recognizing the economic value of having a full time military base close to Jacksonville, formed a committee known as the Air Base Authority to bring the transition to reality. The Authority raised the required $400,000 and offered it to the Armory Board with the proviso that the new National Guard training area be in Duval County or a contiguous county. They delivered a check in the full amount on November 18, 1939. The Authority favored a site northeast of New Berlin, but the Armory Board, desiring a site lending to diversified training, including artillery ranges, selected a site south of State Road 16 in Clay County and approximately 9 miles east of Starke.

Richard P. Daniel, an eminent attorney in Jackson-ville, was retained to acquire the site. A team of professional appraisers was form-ed and approximately 30,000 acres were acquired at a cost of $179,000 (some by negotiation and some by condemnation). The area between State Road 16 and Kingsley Lake was selected as the housing area, and in the last quarter of 1939 work began to make the site a useable training area. The design was for one brigade, with a parade ground centered on the radius of Kingsley Lake. Identical areas were de-signed and constructed on the parade ground consisting of an administrative building, mess halls, latrines and rows of tents.

Work began simultaneously with the salvage of Camp Foster and the clearing of the new encampment area. The only building that was not salvaged at Camp Foster was a portion of the present Navy Exchange. Having a different floor level and architectural treatment than the balance of the Exchange identifies it. WPA labor and Military Department personnel were used for the salvage operation and prisoners from the State Penitentiary at Raiford were used for the clearing operation. Salvaged materials were moved from Camp Foster to the new site using military trucks driven by National Guard personnel. Construction then began using Military Department employees, WPA labor and contractors. A water system and sewage system, including a small disposal plant, came into being and the Florida Power and Light Company furnished electricity.

A telephone line was installed from the camp to the Starke Telephone Company at Starke. Construction was by Military Department personnel and consisted of a pole line carrying two pairs of phantom wires to provide three trunk lines.

With mobilization drawing near, the entire property (except a strip of land along the west boundary between State Road 16 and Kingsley Lake) was leased to the Federal Government and construction was extended to provide facilities for in excess of

Photo: FL. National Guard

Typical Army style barracks erected at Camp Blanding

70,000 personnel. Thus began a mobilization center and training site used by the Army throughout World War II. Its 170,000 acres of scrub oaks and thickets and the training of some 90,000 enlistees at its peak made Camp Blanding the fourth largest city in Florida. Between the war years of 1940-1945, more than 800,000 enlistees and draftees received their military training at Blanding. A Prisoner of War Compound was established east of the service area. It was maintained until the prisoners were repatriated following the war. German and Italian POWs were maintained in separate compounds.

Subsequent to the conclusion of World War II, the Federal Government, through the U.S. Corps of Engineers began to sell the facilities constructed by them incident to mobilization. Their lease with the Armory Board included a restoration clause, and the Armory Board in lieu of restoration retained numerous installations.

The Corps of Engineers decided to declare the lands purchased by the Federal Government (consisting of 40,000 acres) surplus and to sell those lands to private entities. The Armory Board, recognizing the value of that area for training purposes and feeling that the war to end all wars had not yet occurred, decided that the land should be retained for defense purposes.

The entire reservation to include both Federal and state lands was to be held intact in order that it be available for military uses in case of national emergency and the reservation was to be used for military purposes only. Negotiations leading up to the aforementioned agreement were in progress for several months. The agreement was consummated and the deed delivered in 1955.

During the ensuing years, the use of Camp Blanding as a training facility for the Florida National Guard increased significantly, ultimately resulting in its official designation as a National Guard training site by the National Guard Bureau. This designation has facilitated the allotment of Federal funds for operations and maintenance costs and also resulted in the construction of some 160 permanent masonry buildings to house troops while in training. The facility is now used on an almost full-time basis by the National Guard of Florida and the several states, and also by all the active services and their reserve components.

CAMP GORDON JOHNSTON

If Camp Blanding was the largest facility and the fourth largest city in Florida, then Camp Gordon Johnston certainly must have been the largest facility on the Florida Panhandle. It served a unique aspect of the United States Army — amphibious warfare.

At the outbreak of World War II, the armed forces maintained two amphibious corps, one serving the Atlantic Fleet and a second with the Pacific Fleet. The Army viewed these organizations simply as paper organizations. The Navy, with the Marine Corps, maintained a research and training program of amphibious forces. The Army opposed these methods and was not convinced the Navy was capable of training and commanding large numbers of Army units needed for massive invasions.

On April 1942, Army Chief of Staff General George C. Marshall announced that the Army would undergo the planning, preparation and training of ground and Air Corps troops in amphibious warfare. Amphibious training centers were selected and hurried into construction. Camp Edwards, already a training center located on Cape Cod, Massachusetts, was selected as the first site to train troops of divisional size. A smaller site at Ft. Lewis, Washington was selected to train soldiers for the Pacific Theater. Several sites were examined from New Jersey to the Everglades (including Venice, Cedar Key, Caramel and Panama City in Florida) and Bon Secour Bay near Mobile, Alabama. The site selection commission, against considerable opposition, selected the wild area of Carrabelle, Florida.

10,000 acres of scrub land were purchased and another 155,00 acres leased. Site clearing commenced on July 8, 1942. Construction was hurried and mostly completed in sixty days. Although crude, the camp spanned some twenty miles of Gulf coast, between Alligator Point in the east, to St. George Island in the west. In between were the villages of Carrabelle, Carrabelle Beach, Lanark, St. Theresa and Green Point. Four separate camp facilities were constructed, one for the Amphibious Training Center HQ and its support cadre, and the others for the three regimental combat teams that comprised the division. Dog and St. George islands lying just offshore and the various beaches between Alligator Point and St. George's Island were utilized as amphibious landing and training areas. Airborne troops were also trained at Carrabelle as part of the assault forces, and in large regimental numbers.

Originally named Camp Carrabelle, after the town of Carrabelle, it was officially renamed Camp Gordon Johnston in January 1943 after Colonel Johnston, a cavalry officer, who earned the Medal of Honor while fighting in the Philippines during the insurrection.

The first support troops arrived by truck on September 10, 1942. One of these first arrivals was Cpl. James J. Cuffee. He wrote:

I was a career soldier, some three years service in the Army and stationed at Fort Devens, Massachusetts. I was part of a combat engineer cadre, teaching troopers of the 1st and 45th divisions. Then one day, they rounded up a batch of non-commissioned officers and sent us to Camp Carra-belle in Florida. We all thought we had it made — palm trees and warm breezes from the Gulf. None of us knew where Carrabelle was. What a hell hole that was! It was worse than anything I had ever seen, even worse than the CCC camps were. Let me tell you, they were rustic, but this was worse. Latrines were poor and every time it rained, and it did just that most of the time, everything just oozed onto the surface of the ground. It stunk real badly for weeks! My platoon lived in nine-man tents and it was damned cold. Those poor guys in the barracks were no better off, even with pot bellied stoves. Most tents and barracks didn't even have wooden floors or platforms, just dirt. When it rained it was terrible. Everything was mud. Like I said, it was worse than any CCC camp. There we had hot water showers, indoor plumbing and even dining rooms. At Carrabelle, we ate outdoors in the good ole chow line with mess kits. The food was terrible. Yeah, I know the cooks worked wonders with what they had, but it was like that for almost a year, even when the trainees arrived. We even wrote songs about how bad it was. Try this:

Oh the biscuits at Carrabelle,
They say are mighty fine,
One fell off the table,
and killed a pal of mine.

All wash facilities were outdoors with a roof just in case of rain. That was a really bad joke. You either froze or were rained on. It was a long way from Ft. Devens and the simple pleasures we enjoyed there. We spent weeks digging ditches, clearing scrub areas, constructing barracks, mess halls, and finally better latrines and even some rec halls. Everyone was involved and I mean everyone, even guys who couldn't drive a nail. I don't know what those civilian contractors got paid for, but not for what they built. It was just plain shoddy work!

All the time you were working, those stinking chiggers, sand flies or mosquitoes ate you alive. I think the chiggers were the worse insects I had ever met. They got in where your clothing fit tight, like around your belt and feasted on your blood. I used to rub ammonia water on me to take away the itch, an old trick a mountain man taught me in Montana, but my pals didn't care for the smell. When they found out how well it worked, we all smelled like ammonia. One day at inspection, the Company Commander wanted to know why we all smelled like ammonia. We told him, and the next day even he smelled like the rest of the company. I tell you it was no picnic living with chiggers.

When we got through with building Camp #3, where I was, they started us on the training mock-ups, such as cargo net towers so we could teach troopers how to disembark a ship and load the land craft. We constructed obstacle courses, pill boxes and all kinds of beach defenses. We also constructed live-fire obstacle courses and realistic street fighting set ups.

Then there were the rattlesnakes! Once you killed off most of them, work went a lot easier. They seemed to be just about everywhere, just like the wild hogs. But the hogs provided some sport — at least we could shoot them. We always kept a few Springfield rifles nearby. When someone yelled "Hogs" we'd grab the rifles and shoot. We Northerners didn't dare eat the dirty porkers, but those gentlemen from the South feasted on them. To each his own.

The boys of the 38th Infantry Division arrived about the tail end of November and went directly into training. Let me tell you, training was not always glorious. There simply was no equipment, not even rifles. There were many troopers who were outfitted with a broomstick handle or wooden rifle made by one of the many woodworking shops. At first there were not even tanks, just large signs with the red lettering of tank. Nor were there landing

Photo: US Navy

Amphibious landing drills by the US Army at Camp Gordon Johnston

craft. Even the explosives for the live-fire exercises were lacking. We wondered if the big brass would ever get their acts together.

It took a while, but we finally got most of what material we needed and eventually it was a glorious sight. LCVPs (Landing Craft Vehicle Personnel), LCVPRs, LCTRs, LCTs and LCIs were all used in training small craft crews as well as placing soldiers into what seemed like actual combat conditions. There were explosions and smoke just about everywhere. Very realistic.

The 38th left at the end of December and was replaced by the 28th Infantry Division, commanded by Omar Bradley. Never saw the man myself, but hear tell he thoroughly enjoyed himself. I recall the 28th as the last of the division-sized units to train at Carrabelle. Oh yes, the place was renamed for some Civil War Colonel, Gordon Johnston, I believe. We still called the place by a number of names, but mostly Carrabelle.

After the 28th left we trained special regimental combat teams for amphibious assaults. I was transferred to Ft. Pierce and became part of a combat engineer platoon. They also promoted me to Sergeant which made me happy. On March 5, 1943, we were shipped to England in time to go ashore at Normandy, the day after the invasion. I was still glad to have left Camp Johnston.

Camp Gordon Johnston formally closed down on June 10, 1943 but in September 1943 it was re-designated as an Army Service Forces Training Center (ASF). With the increase of fighting in the Pacific, amphibious forces were greatly needed. The new amphibious training centered on the use of the new amphibious truck, the DUKW, the so-called *DUCK*. Late in 1942, the amphibious truck, all wheeled and provided with power takeoff drive to power a propeller shaft, could travel over the water at a speed of 6-8 miles per hour. It was used to unload ships moored in harbors but not tied to a dock. It could then propel itself through the water onto the beach, unload and return for more cargo.

When the war ended, the number of troops stationed at Camp Gordon Johnston declined rapidly and the military closed the base in 1946. The government disposed of all properties and returned some 37,000 acres of land to the St. Joe Paper Co.

James J. Cuffee again: *I went back a few years ago, with my wife and two grandchildren and couldn't find a trace of the place. It was a pesthole, but it was our pesthole. I miss it. Hope they never build another like it!*

Chapter Three

The Army Air Bases

Defense activity was being rushed long. The Japanese brought the United States completely into World War II. New Army and Navy installations were being constructed throughout Florida. Thousands of servicemen came to Florida to train and staff the new facilities. Camp Blanding was being rushed to handle the thousands of inductees and draftees.

Army airfields at Drew and MacDill fields in Tampa allowed more new recruit pilots to be trained. Eglin Field at Valparaiso geared up as a much-needed proving ground for new aircraft and weapons. British Royal Air Force cadets were arriving at air training schools such as Carlstrom at Arcadia and at the University of Miami.

Military tradition placed pilot training in Texas, where the weather remained suitable. Enough space existed in Texas to meet the expanded demands of the rapidly growing Army Air Force. However, politics, that fine art of compromise or arm-twisting, influenced the Army to build many needed airfields in Florida.

In addition to the strong lobbying by the senior Senator from Florida, Claude Pepper, local governments lobbied the armed forces to build their new bases within their communities. Incentives of real estate, recently upgraded municipal airports or new ones built in conjunction with the Civil Aeronautics Administration (CAA), were offered.

Competition quickly developed between the Army and the Navy for the most desirable land sites for airfields. The airfield building program of the Army started a year before that of the Navy and generally resulted in many being little utilized and unused. The Navy program tended to concentrate its facilities and schools, such as NAS Pensacola and NAS Jacksonville.

The Army built airfields, which generally followed a predictable design, a large C-shaped ramp, surrounded by three or four runways. Local municipal airports or fields designed for light aircraft were upgraded and used as emergency landing fields or as temporary training fields. These support or emergency airfields were generally listed by the Army as auxiliary airfields. Unlike the Navy, the Army rarely dedicated any of the airfields in honor of former Army Air Force aviators. Names were generally borrowed from the community such as with Venice Airfield.

Airfields also served as sites for various air corps service-training groups. For example — gunnery instructors school at Buckingham Field (at Fort Myers), engine maintenance at Venice Field and combat support groups at MacDill.

Until quarters, barracks, service shops, schools and dispensaries were in place, life for base crews was basic and rugged. They were housed in winterized tents and slept on canvas cots with no mattresses. Despite the many hardships, the white sandy beaches played a role in keeping morale high. Many of the personnel stationed at these many training bases remembered the delightful weather and miles of extraordinary beaches and returned after the war to either live or vacation in Florida.

The past history of these Army airfields is long forgotten by many and unknown to the young. Volunteers maintain this fragile link to the past by collecting and documenting local histories. This book would not be possible without their remarkable work. Nineteen Army bases have been selected and their brief histories documented in order to give the reader some idea of the role they played in training pilots and crews to fight in the air war of World War II.

AVON PARK ARMY AIRFIELD, AVON

When Colonel Clint T. Johnson assumed command of the Avon Park Army Airfield on November 7, 1942, he was ordered to direct the completion of all base construction. In addition to supervisory duties of the airfield, Col. Johnson supervised the construction and opening of the new practice bombing range for the training of bombardiers, pilots and bomber crews destined for overseas combat, especially the European Theater of war.

The Avon Park Airfield bombing range was not only the biggest of its kind in size, but it possessed one of the most unique practice bombing layouts in the world. The range sprawled over some 220,000 acres or about 343 square miles of typical central Florida pinewoods. This vast area contained seven target ranges — a water area that contained a full-scale mock-up of a Japanese submarine, a miniature city complete with city streets, oil and gas storage tanks, warehouses, lights, docks and ships all designed for aircraft high altitude missions. It also contained a railway moving target which included an enormous figure-eight track layout, complete with remote controlled locomotive and car targets. A strafing target consisted of a simulated airfield with aircraft in different takeoff positions.

On December 9, 1943, the name Avon Park Bombing Range was officially changed to Avon Park Army Airfield. A request to Army Headquarters in Washington, DC for permission to name the new field after a World War II hero was denied.

The Avon Park base was officially activated on October 5, 1942. It is located 10 miles eastnorth east of Avon Park and is partly situated in Polk County and Highland County. The base was placed on inactive status by the Third Air Force HQ on October 1, 1945. Since that date it has been placed once again on the active status.

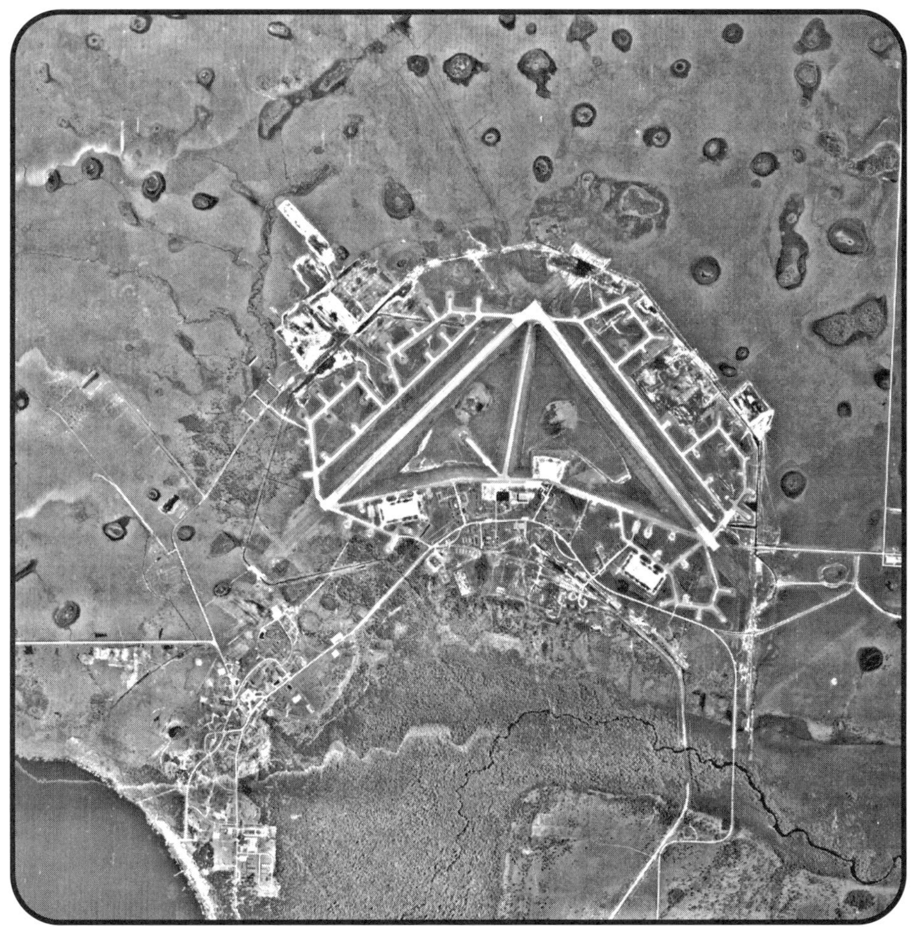

Photo: US Air Force

Aerial view of Avon Park bombing range and airfield

BARTOW AAF, BARTOW

Early in 1942 the municipal airport at Bartow consisted of a rough airstrip operated for small private single-engine aircraft. Beginning with the present site of Murphy Chevrolet Co. the airfield ran about half a mile west, parallel to Route 60. The airstrip was unable to accommodate heavy commercial or military aircraft.

C.E. Williams, a local businessman and city commissioner persuaded the city of Bartow to purchase 900 acres of phosphate land and offer it to the U.S. Army. The Civil Aviation Administration and the Army examined the site and approved. Construction work on the airfield began immediately. The constant need for pilot training sites helped promote the Bartow site.

Several thousand construction workers swarmed about the area rushing to build the new airstrip, barracks and the vast assortment of support buildings. Before construction was completed a training cadre from Third Air Force, MacDill Air Base at Tampa arrived and established a training program. Army pilots were trained quickly and soon a constant drone of aircraft filled the skies over Bartow. Training planes, such as the Stearman biplane, were constantly in the air during daylight hours. Since little night flying instruction was given student pilots, few planes bothered the area at night.

The airfield was at first designated an Army Auxiliary Airfield, then as an Auxiliary Training Field. The name for the city became the name of the airfield.

As the war progressed and the need for pilot training was diminished, training planes were replaced by small numbers of updated fighter aircraft. Eventually an auxiliary field named Armour was constructed to support the Bartow Airfield. The Bartow base continued to serve MacDill as an emergency field until the end of the war. In 1946 the airfield reverted to the city of Bartow.

Photo: Bartow Historical Library

Aerial view of Bartow training airfield, Bartow

BOCA RATON AAF, BOCA RATON

In early 1942, General "Hap" Arnold came to Florida seeking a site to establish a school to train Army personnel in the new technique of radar. Three sites were investigated. After a careful investigation it was decided to build at Boca Raton. Many residents and absentee-tourist landlords resisted the idea fearing that they would be moved from their land and homes.

By May of 1942, the Army had officially acquired 5,820 acres of land. With some 3,500 construction workers and an infusion of $11 million, the Boca Raton Air Base was completed within four months. Cadre troops began occupying the field in August of 1942. The field was officially commissioned October 15, 1942. The base continued to grow eventually reaching 16,000 troops by 1945.

Some of the best technical minds from around the country came to experiment and teach about the new device called "radar." This rader was not designed for static ground use but for aircraft, especially heavy bombers.

As the war progressed and the school's training program developed, more and more aircraft were assigned to the Boca Raton airfield. In the beginning, old dilapidated bombers were assigned radar training duties. Later more modern aircraft, such as the B-24s, B-17s, B-26s and the B-25s were utilized. The heavy offshore shipping traffic was ideal for radar-guided bombers to track and practice bomb runs. The Boca Raton pilots often made radar bomb runs on the vast Avon Park bombing range, further honing their skills.

Boca Raton was the Army Air Force's only radar training facility during World War II. The training station provided airmen with a variety of instructions, which included electronics, radar operation and maintenance mechanics. During this time only officers were trained in electronics.

On June 27, 1949, the town of Boca Raton offered the Army $251,284 for the airfield and all its properties, bringing to a close this military presence.

Photo: Boca Raton Historical Society

Boca Raton medium bomber training airfield

BROOKSVILLE AAF, BROOKSVILLE

A board of commissioned officers was designated by Headquarters, Third Air Force, to investigate land offered by the town of Brooksville as a training airfield. The Army's need for the immediate construction of the field far outweighed any economic consideration at the time. It was estimated that approximately $20,875 would cover the cost of the 2,014 acres.

The site selected was 7.5 miles southwest of Brooksville in Hernando County, lying west of U.S. Highway 41. It had excellent drainage, adequate water supply and it was large enough to build the standard Army training airfield — three runways that would be suitable for heavy bombers, taxiways and hard stands for the aircraft. The facilities would provide for approximately 2,000 to 3,000 officers and others.

Approval was quickly given on May 1, 1942 and construction began at once. Hangars, barracks and other support buildings and facilities were rushed into construction, as the clearing of the airfield proceeded. A small training cadre arrived to supervise the establishment of the facility and by the time the air base was complete, a staff of about 2,000 personnel occupied the base.

The 9th Bombardment Group trained at Brooksville with B-17s and B-24s. The 9th Bombardment Group consisted of the 1st, 5th, 99th and 490th Bomb Squadrons. The 1st Bomb Squadron arrived on November 15, 1942. The 338th Service Maintenance Group arrived at Brooksville in early January 1943.

The 1159th School Squadron arrived at

Photo: John Flynn

The flight line at Brooksville Airfield 1943.

Brooksville in January of 1944. The airfield served primarily as a heavy bomber-training base, with daily runs to various target and bombardment sites. Many of the B-17 and B-24 crews became well acquainted with the Avon Park Range and the bombing range at Osprey.

The 3rd Bomber Command at MacDill Field was given command of Brooksville AAF and assigned it as an auxiliary base to Drew Field. Brooksville Army Airfield was officially decommissioned by the Army in late 1945 and, after considered arrangements, returned to the town of Brooksville.

BUCKINGHAM ARMY AIRFIELD, FORT MYERS

In February 1942 Lt. Col. W.A. Maxwell was flown to Fort Myers from Tyndal AFB to meet with the mayor, city officials and county commissioners. Maxwell indicated the Army Air Corps needed to establish two army air bases in the area. They discussed the use of Page Field, the Fort Myers Civil Airport, and approximately 75,000 acres of land at Buckingham located northeast of the Fort Myers area. The Buckingham field was to be developed for a flexible gunnery school in order to train men to handle 50-caliber turrets and waist guns for heavy bombers such as the B-17 and B-24.

In March 1942, 650 men arrived to begin construction of the facility. The field was officially activated July 5, 1942. Training began on September 5th as soon as the runways were completed. A total of 483 buildings were erected, including seven mess halls, one hangar, 228 barracks and 24 hospital buildings. The range facilities included a 1,000-inch machine gun range, a skeet range, a moving target range and Waller Trainers.

Most of the training schools within the Army Air Force Eastern Flying Training Command had several auxiliary fields which were used for flight training operations at those stations. Thirty-six

Photo: Fort Myers Historical Museum

Heavy bomber training facility at Buckingham Army Airfield, Fort Myers

miles below Fort Myers on the Gulf, Naples became the site for the second new airfield, with two 4,000-ft. runways. The bombing range was located at the north end of the Fort Myers beach, four miles off-shore and extending 85 miles north to Shark Point and some 40 miles in width. Present day Marco and Sanibel islands were used by the heavy bombers as bombing and machine gun ranges. Tow planes with target sleeves flew parallel to the beaches with aerial gunners shooting 100 rounds of live ammunition with each run up the beach.

B-17s from Hendrick's Field, Sebring and Sarasota used the shore ranges along the west coast during the early part of 1942. At the end of the war Buckingham was deactivated and the site was returned to the city of Fort Myers.

EGLIN AAF, VALPARAISO

Eglin Army Air Force Base (the name then) is located on the Florida Panhandle, facing Choctawhatchee Bay a few miles from the open waters of the Gulf of Mexico. Situated about fifty miles east of Pensacola and just west of the two communities of Niceville and Valparaiso.

The Army needed to establish an Air Corps Proving Ground necessary for the testing of aircraft armaments and equipment. At the time such work was being performed at the Aberdeen Proving Grounds in Maryland. Search had begun early, seeking a site suitable for a bombing and gunnery range. Valparaiso was a small resort community situated on the edge of the Choctawhatchee National Forest. The businessmen of Valparaiso realized the commercial advantage of a large military installation. In 1933 a small municipal airport was established. In 1935 Maxwell Field, Alabama leased the airport as the Headquarters for an air base. In 1937 the military reservation at Valparaiso was designated as Eglin Field in honor of Lt. Col. Frederick I. Eglin, a member of the Air Corps Tactical School, killed in a line of duty crash in Alabama.

During the war in Europe, 1910, Eglin Field was re-designated as an Air Corps Specialized Flying School. The Air Corps Proving was established in May 19, 1911. The 23rd Composite Group arrived from Orlando to provide flight-testing programs. Auxiliary fields were established at nearby sites as training fields or emergency airfields. The airfield at Niceville was commissioned Eglin 82, Crestview became Eglin #3, Garnier, Eglin 14 and so on for a total of ten auxiliary airfields. Eglin is now an Air Force base.

The Eglin Gulf Test Range covers 4,000 square miles of Gulf water. The Armament Division of the Air Force Systems Command comprises an area of 720 square miles, or about two-thirds the size of Rhode Island. Today Eglin serves as a proving ground for the latest military aviation technology with a military and civilian force of about 14,000.

Photo: Smithsonian Institute

Flight training facility at Eglin Army Air Force Base near Valparaiso

HENDRICKS AAF, SEBRING

In 1940 citrus crops, cattle ranching and tourism formed the main economy base of Sebring in Highlands County. Early in 1941 Army Air Corps personnel arrived on the scene, with the objective of examining the area for a possible air base for heavy bombers. In June 1941, Sebring officials received the news authorizing 9,200 acres of land to serve as an Air Corps base to train pilots and crews of bombers. Construction commenced the next month in July. A railroad spur had to be constructed on an access road to SR 59. Crews worked preparing the site 24 hours a day. On January 8, 1942 post HQ moved its personnel into permanent structures. On January 14, 1942 the Basic Flying School was officially named Hendricks Army Air Field, after 1st Lt. Woodruff Hendricks, Jr., a native of Florida who died while on duty in England.

The first heavy bomber, a B-17, arrived at Hendricks Field on January 29, 1942. The first class of the Combat Crew School graduated April 15, 1942. To say that Hendricks was a busy place is to understate the situation. Over 7,000 takeoffs and landings by B-17s were not at all unusual within a single week. A total complement consisted of 225 officers and nurses and 2,456 enlisted men. Reports indicate that sometime in 1943, 80 WACS became part of the base personnel, serving in a variety of positions.

In the early stages of the war some of the B-17s from Hendricks Field flew daily submarine patrol along the Atlantic coast of Florida. Carrying the standard 500-lb. depth charge, a few planes were

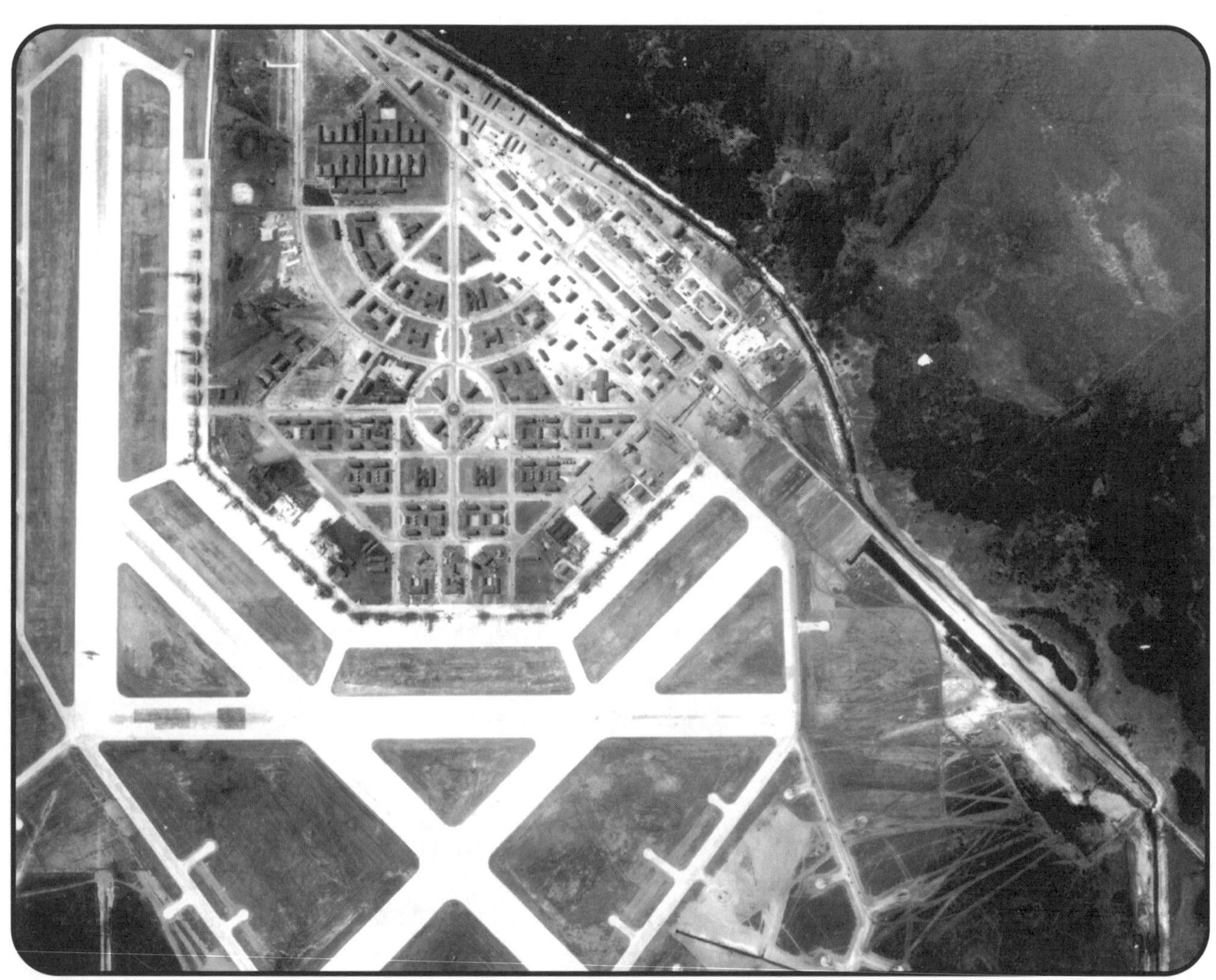

Photo: Smithsonian Institute

Heavy bomber training field at Hendricks Army Airfield, Sebring

officially recorded as having damaged German U-boats.

Bombardiers and crew gunners were kept busy firing at tow targets at the Naples Range and Avon Park Range. Many a nearby town would suddenly discover it had been unexpectedly bombed by an errant sandbag or two. On May 1, 1946 Sebring took over operation and possession and made the field into an industrial park complex. The world famous Sebring 12-hour Grand Prix Endurance Race is held here each year.

HOMESTEAD AAF, HOMESTEAD

Homestead Air Force Base is tucked away at the southern end of the Florida peninsula, between the Everglades National Park and Miami. The air base is located five miles east of Homestead.

On September 16, 1942, the Caribbean Wing, Air Transport Command at Morrison Field, West Palm Beach, assumed command of the recently constructed Homestead Base. In keeping with many other Florida communities, the good citizens of Homestead purchased land and offered its use as an Army air base. When construction of the usual three intersecting runways, hangars and support buildings had been completed, an HQ cadre from Morrison Field at nearby West Palm Beach moved in to commence operations.

The original intent, as was the dominant need, was to provide a field for the rapid training of pilots. Due to the near isolated setup of the station and its primary function as a training site, it was decided to direct the overflow of overseas aircraft that could not be handled by other stations of the Caribbean Wing. With the war in Europe raging, the need for more and more aircraft increased. The 54th Ferrying Squadron of the Caribbean Wing's 15th Ferrying Group was stationed at Homestead. It was the 54th's responsibility to see that planes of all types, fighters and bombers, were ferried from

Photo: Florida Pioneer Museum

Aerial view of Homestead Army Airfield, Homestead

Photo: Florida pioneer Museum

Repair and Stowage hangars at Homestead Army Airfield, Homestead

Homestead to the Middle East. The route generally took them south to South America, to Eastern Africa then on to battle areas of North Africa or on to India and China.

The hurricane of 1945 destroyed the facility and caused the base to be temporarily closed. Once again a hurricane, Andrew, temporarily closed the base in 1992.

LAKELAND AAF, LAKELAND

Among the many sites chosen for airfields by the Army was the airport constructed by the CAA during the summer of 1942 for the city of Lakeland. Originally it was intended to serve as a municipal airport. After the addition of more land, the Army Corps of Engineers greatly enlarged the field. It was then designed as an operational training field for heavy bombers such as the B-17 and the B-24. It became known as Drane Field.

The Lakeland Municipal Airport was officially designated as Lakeland Field #2 on September 12, 1942. It was to serve as an auxiliary base to MacDill in Tampa.

It was located about six miles southwest of the city of Lakeland. It was constructed in the usual Army fashion of three intersecting runways at the center. This arrangement made it difficult for planes to land while others were taking off.

Five squadrons of the 98th Bombardment Group were housed and trained at the field, as well as the 4th Weather Squadron. The 98th used the various Tampa gunnery and bombing ranges, including the one located at Osprey. In its final bomb-training program, Avon Park became the center of training.

The Lakeland School of Aeronautics operated a training field at Eaton Park, which was owned and operated by Albert I. Lodwick. The school was one of the contract schools used to train pilots. When first started, the school was used to train American fliers, but as the need for more British pilots increased, it was switched to training RAF pilot cadets.

Three airfields existed in Lakeland during the war: (1) Lakeland Army Air Base at the former Lakeland Municipal Airport; (2) the Haldeman-Elder, known as Eaton Park, which served the Lodwick training school; and (3) Lakeland Army Airfield which served as a bomber training facility and as an emergency airstrip for nearby airfields, including MacDill.

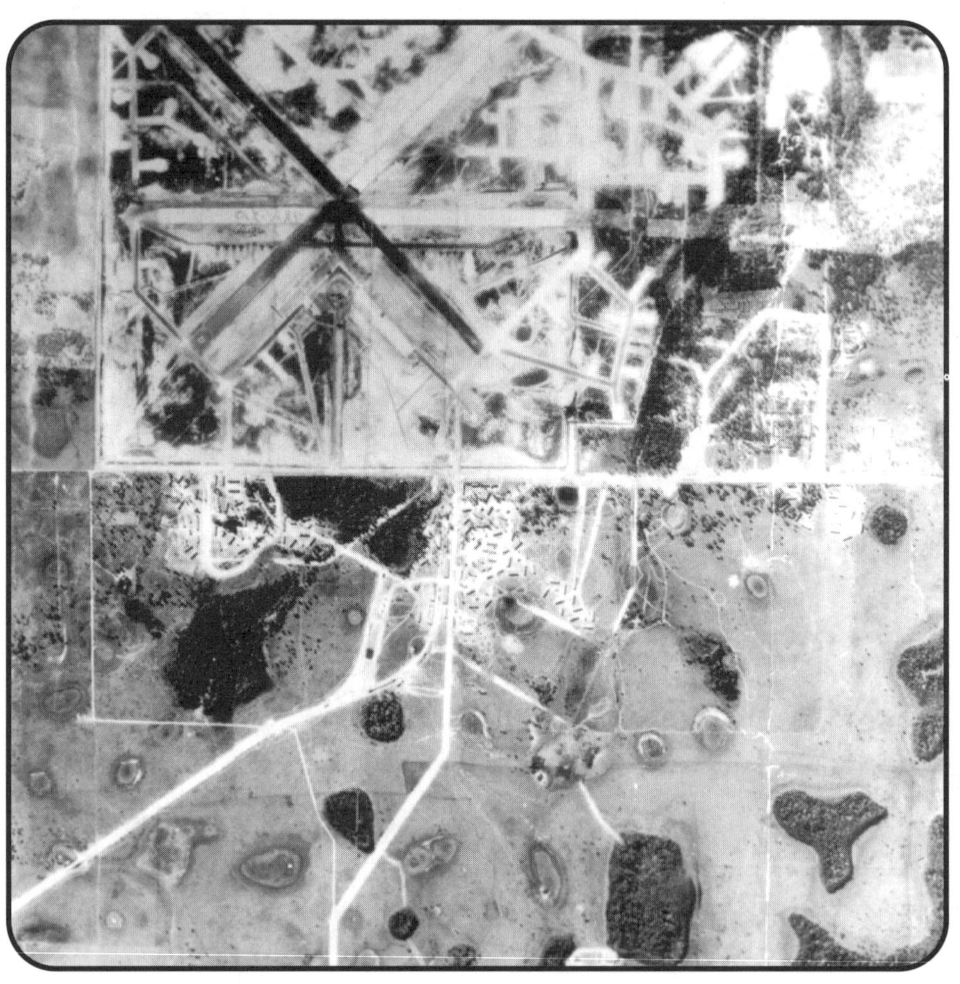

Photo: Smithsonian Institute

Aerial view of Lakeland Army air training facility, Lakeland

MacDill Army Air Base, Tampa

In January 1939, a Federal commission was appointed by the War Department to seek locations for six new airfields, which included one to be located in the southeastern United States. A Mayor's committee composed of leading businessmen from the Tampa area was organized to lobby for the southeast air base. Eventually Tampa Bay was picked as the site for the new air base. It was to be located on land known locally as Catfish Point.

Hillsborough County acquired 3,500 acres of land, then donated it to the government, while 2,900 acres of land were to be acquired by the War Department. Soon thereafter in November 1939 the WPA assigned men to clear nearly 5,800 acres of scrub land. Very quickly, despite Army Air Corps general policy, the new field was named for Col. Leslie MacDill. Col. MacDill was a promising officer when his career was cut short at age 48 when he died in an accident.

Official dedication occurred on April 15, 1941. With just three runways, the new MacDill Army Airfield was to serve as a transitional training facility. Flying cadres from the 29th and 44th Bombardment Group instructed replacement-training units which flew the B-17s.

Three major airfields (including MacDill) were located in Tampa during the war. Henderson Field was located where Busch Gardens is today. Drew Field was situated where the present Tampa International Airport is located. Both airfields served as auxiliary operational support bases for MacDill. Zephryhills, Brooksville and other fields peripheral to MacDill served as training and auxiliary fields. Mullet Key, Terra Ceia, South Venice and

Photo: Smithsonian Instutute

Located at Catfish Point, Tampa, MacDill Army Air Base served as a transitional training facility for heavy bombers.

Osprey provided large gunnery and bombing ranges. During the war, some 15,000 troops were stationed at MacDill, and a large contingent of WACS served from 1943 in a variety of positions. Different bombardment groups outfitted and trained at MacDill then departed for overseas. Early in March of 1945 R-29s arrived to undergo training and shakedown. After the war, MacDill Army Air Base remained an operational facility for SAC, the Strategic Air Command.

MARIANNA ARMY AIR BASE, MARIANNA

The Pilot Training Command at Maxwell AAF cast about for an airfield to be used for advanced single-engine training. Advanced single-engine aircraft consisted of monoplane trainers called AT-6s. Ideally situated, Marianna is located on the Florida Panhandle between Pensacola and Tallahassee. A land of heavily wooded rolling hills, it is unlike the flat palm and pine covered landscape of southern Florida.

They located the base five miles northeast of State Highway 90 outside the city of Marianna. During the summer the Army brass from Maxwell Air Force's Southeast Training Command visited the area and concluded an arrangement whereby the airstrip at Marianna would be leased to the Army Air Force for the duration of the war. During the summer of 1942 construction workers labored to modify the existing airstrip into a three intersecting runways airfield. Hangars and support buildings were quickly erected and the field was commissioned in early fall.

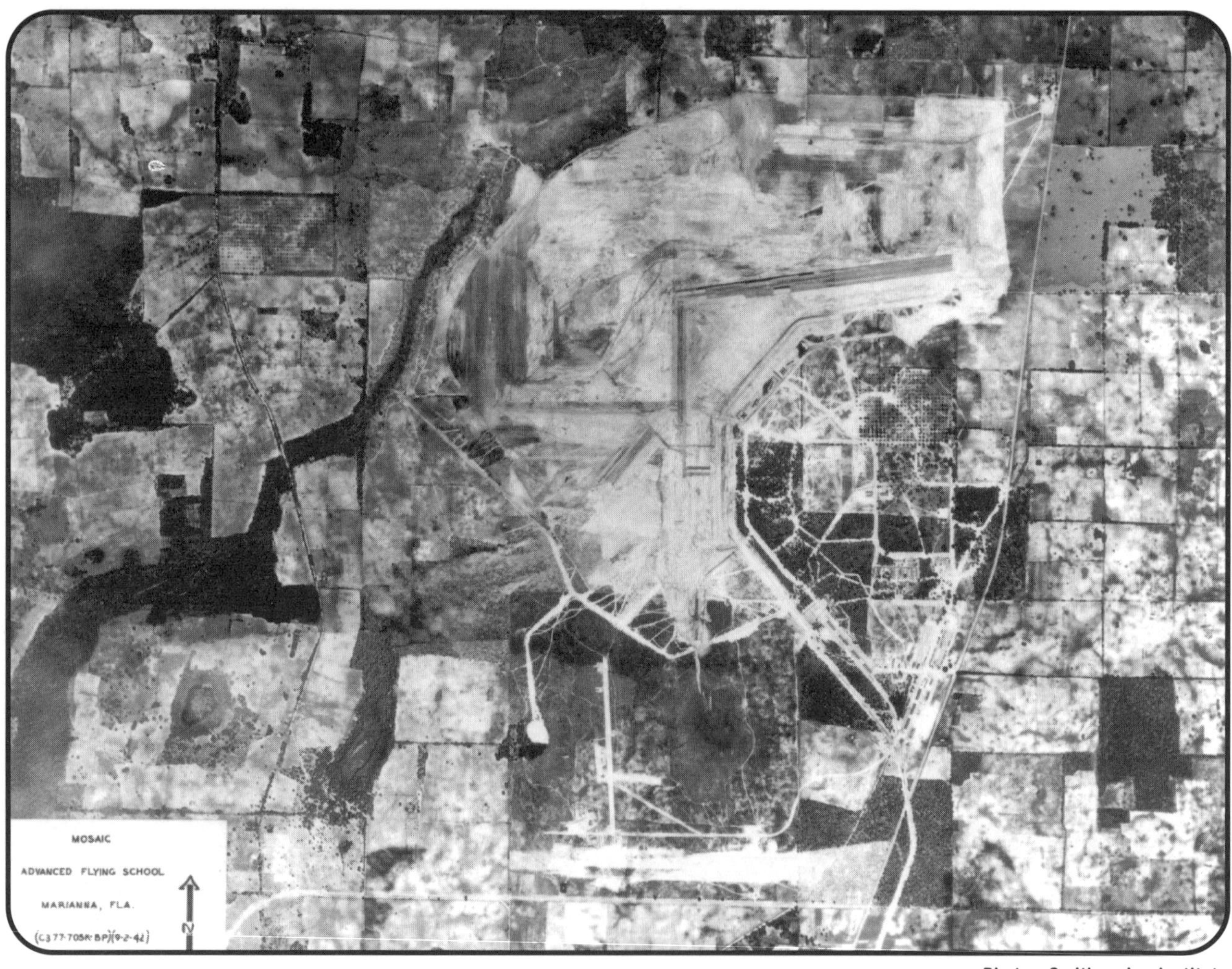

Photo: Smithsonian Institute

Aerial view of Marianna Army Airfield, a flight training Facility, at Marianna

A training cadre was sent from Maxwell AAF (Montgomery, Alabama) and soon thereafter AT-6 trainers began to arrive via the Ferry Command. Class sizes generally numbered one hundred and several classes might be training at one time. This created not only an air traffic problem, but placed a strain on housing and maintenance crews. It was not long before additional auxiliary training fields had to be selected and constructed.

Altogether five auxiliary airfields were built or used within a 15-mile radius of Marianna. Ellis #1 was also used for training purposes and as an auxiliary to Marianna. Malone #2, about 15 miles north of Marianna, Bascom #3 and Alliance #4 all served as training and auxiliary fields. All fields were constructed to handle fighter type aircraft. Fighter planes from nearby Tyndall and Eglin air bases also used these fields as emergency airstrips. All these fields reverted to their respective communities at the end of the war with the Army Air Base becoming the Marianna Municipal Airport.

MORRISON AAF, WEST PALM BEACH

The 313th Material Squadron was activated on October 30, 1941, and served at the Miami Municipal Airport. The Squadron performed first and second echelons maintenance on all Army and Allied aircraft ferried through the Miami Airport. After negotiations to expand the facility at Miami failed, the entire squadron was transferred to Morrison Field at West Palm Beach.

A tent camp was quickly put in place to house the sudden increase in troops. Shortly after their arrival in April 1942 a severe rainstorm flooded Morrison Field, covering the area with 3 to 4 feet of water. Needless to say the tent containment was destroyed.

In addition to maintaining aircraft of the Ferry Command, duties also consisted of handling all air cargo and maintaining all airport facilities. The Air Engineers Section utilized the two aircraft hangars which belonged to the Palm Beach Aero Club.

The winter of 1943 and 1944 saw the heaviest traffic in aircraft pass through Morrison Field since organizing the base. Ferry planes were overhauled, repaired and tested for airworthiness. Two test pilots, Lts. Stanker and Bushnell, had the responsibility of testing aircraft after major overhauls were performed and that was often.

Various dignitaries inspected this all-important facility, among them the Duke of Windsor. Prince Bernhardt of the Netherlands had his aircraft repaired by a crew from the 313th. He expressed his personal thanks for their efficient work.

The overseas demand for military aircraft of all types in 1942 was so great that the 1,000 men at Morrison worked three shifts, seven days a week, to keep planes in the Ferry Command pipeline.

As part of the overall command structure of Ferry Command, a cadre was sent from Morrison to Homestead to train and maintain aircraft. It is recorded that some 250 WACS served at Morrison in all capacities.

Photo: US Air Force

Aerial view of Morrison Army Airfield, West Palm Beach
The 313th Materiel Squadron was based here during the war.

PAGE FIELD AAF, FORT MYERS

When the Army Air Corps took command of the Lee County Airport in 1942, the County Commission changed the name of the airport to Page Field. The field was so named in honor of Channing Page, a Fort Myers lad who was a World War I ace.

Page Field was a large dual-purpose base, consisting of fighter planes and heavy bombers. Graduates of the Army Air Force flight schools in Florida were taught to use the pursuit fighter planes of the day. The average stay at Page Field was approximately three months, during which time pilots logged about 60 hours of flight time. Typical fighters that were stationed at Page were the P-39, P-40, P-47 and the famed P-51s. The P-39, although not well received by the American airmen, was beloved by the Russians and hundreds were sold to the Soviets via the Lend Lease program. Russian flight instructors were trained at Page field.

Early in April 1942 the 98th Bombardment Group began its training program, shooting at moving and stationary targets along coastal gunnery ranges. Soon they were making bomb runs on the same beaches using 100 lb. sandfilled practice bombs. Upon completion of training, the 98th was transferred to the Middle East, to be replaced by the 93rd Bombardment Group.

The air base was crowded by a large population of palmetto palms and soon it was being called "Palmetto Field." The mosquito problem was very acute and anyone not sleeping under a mosquito net was seriously affected. A drainage program for standing water, some controlled chemical treatment and the use of the traditional mosquito repellent solved most of the pesky problem.

Photo: Fort Myers Historical Museum

Aerial View of Page Field at Fort Myers

Photo: Fort Myers Historical Museum

A training flight line of P-39s located at Page Field at Fort Myers

At the peak of World War II some four thousand men and women were stationed at Page Field. Upon completion of training elsewhere, pilots and ground personnel were formed into fighter squadrons or bomber squadrons, trained and then sent to overseas bases.

At the end of World War II Page Field reverted to Fort Myers and Lee County and became the Lee County Municipal Airport.

ORLANDO AAF, ORLANDO

In October of 1939 the Orlando Air School, became an approved agency for the Civilian Pilot Training program (CPT). Orlando provided free ground school to accepted college students and free flight training for students in the upper 10% of their classes. The cost was picked up by the Army. The cadets were taught by experienced civilian instructors. They received their basic training prior to their advanced training at training facilities conducted by the Army. The Orlando Air School came under the command of the Army Air Corps Technical Training Command (AAFTTC), Number 4. The air school was at first a small part of the Orlando Municipal Airport.

In 1942, the U.S. Army Air Combat Control Squadron #2, an amphibious group, selected Orlando as its training facility. It was soon followed by Amphibious Squadron #1. This increase of personnel and aircraft placed a burden on the air school and the airfield. Auxiliary fields were quickly established at Pine Castle about 7 miles southeast of Orlando. Cannon Mills, a field that really served the

Photo: Smithsonian Institute

Orlando Army Airfield training facility, Orlando

air training group was located 4 miles northeast of Orlando. The small strip at Holquist was also utilized as an emergency strip.

Rollins College at Winter Park, located about 5 to 7 miles north of Orlando, operated a flight training school for the CPT. Rollins College utilized the Orlando auxiliary fields as part of its training programs, especially when emergencies arose.

All cadets received about 45 hours total flying time, primarily in the PT-17 Stearman. Unlike many Army pilot training facilities, the primary training schools provided several hours of night and instrument flight time.

Eventually the Army closed down its presence at Orlando and the airfield returned to the civil authorities. The Navy, however, set up a basic training "boot camp" facility and allied Navy schools.

PINELLAS AAF, ST. PETERSBURG

Shortly after the United States entered World War II, civic leaders in the "Sunshine City," St. Petersburg, like many other depression-ridden communities, sought out the military. Early in 1942 representatives from the Army arrived and determined that St. Petersburg, being close by MacDill, would be an ideal training facility for new pilots. The Government secured leases for four small airports, hotels and many parcels of open parkland.

Four air bases were in use during the war within the city area of St. Petersburg. The Army Air Corps quickly enlarged and occupied the Albert Whitted Field which was located along side Rayboro Harbor with the Maritime Service Base and War Shipping Administration. The Pinellas County Municipal Airport became an Army Air Base for the training of fighter pilots. The P-39 with its tricycle landing gear was a common sight sitting on the runways. Construction of Pinellas County Municipal Airport was in progress when the Army assumed command. After lengthening the runways, erecting a control tower and building barracks to house 1,500 pilot trainees, the Army began training in August 1942.

The Albert Whitted Field was turned over to the Navy who in turn allowed the Coast Guard to maintain an air base and boat facility. In 1939 the Coast Guard began to operate an air station at Whitted and with its small number of aircraft flying anti-sub missions, it also operated an air-sea rescue station at Bayboro Harbor. This site served as the first home of the present day Eckerd College. The airfield also served as an emergency field. The Navy utilized the Piper-Fuller Field as an emergency field to Albert Whitted and as a training field.

Mullet Key served as the Air Corps' main gunnery and bombing range. Swarms of B-17s, B-25s, B-26s and smaller aircraft made daily flying practice missions over the barrier islands of the Keys.

Photo: St. Petersburg Museum of History

Aerial view of Pinellas Army Airfield at St. Petersburg

Photo: St. Petersburg Museum of History

Flight line of P-40 trainers at Pinellas Army Airfield

PUNTA GORDA AAF, PUNTA GORDA

Punta Gorda is located next to the Peace River, east of Port Charlotte on Route 41. During World War II, at the instigation of Senator Claude Pepper and local businessmen, the Army constructed an airfield at Punta Gorda. It became a sub-base for the Sarasota Army Air Force base on September 4, 1943. Subsequently, effective March 1, 1944, it was relieved as a sub-base of Sarasota and reassigned as a sub-base of the Venice Army Air Base in Venice, under the command of Colonel V. B. Dixon. It was designated the 344th AAF Base Unit.

An east-to-west runway, one hundred and fifty feet wide by five thousand feet in length, was hurried into construction. A second and third runway were constructed to form the usual Army intersection of three runways. Hardstands were also constructed to support a variety of fighter aircraft.

An assortment of wooden buildings and structures were constructed — 268 huts, wooden floors, walls for pyramid tents, support building and a 20-foot CAA tower and support building. The base detachment consisted of the 27th Service Group sent from the Venice Army Air Base. It took over the daily command of the field. 163 enlisted men and 23 officers made up the 27th Service Group as well as 10 enlisted men and 2 officers of the Weather Station Detail. Punta Gorda was to serve as a fighter replacement training facility. Soon after commissioning ceremonies, P-47 fighter planes arrived and training began.

Pilots that completed the course were immediately shipped to wherever they would be needed as replacement combat pilots. Eventually the famed P-51 Mustang made its appearance in Punta Gorda and attracted considerable attention. Hotshot pilots were known to buzz local cattle ranches as well as the airfield.

The 502 Fighter-Bomber Squadron and the 490th Fighter Squadron trained at Punta Gorda. Both squadrons did their share at shooting up the gunnery ranges at Naples. At the end of the war the airfield reverted to the city of Punta Gorda.

Photo: Punta Gorda Historical Society

Tent area for flight repair crews at Punta Gorda Army Airfield

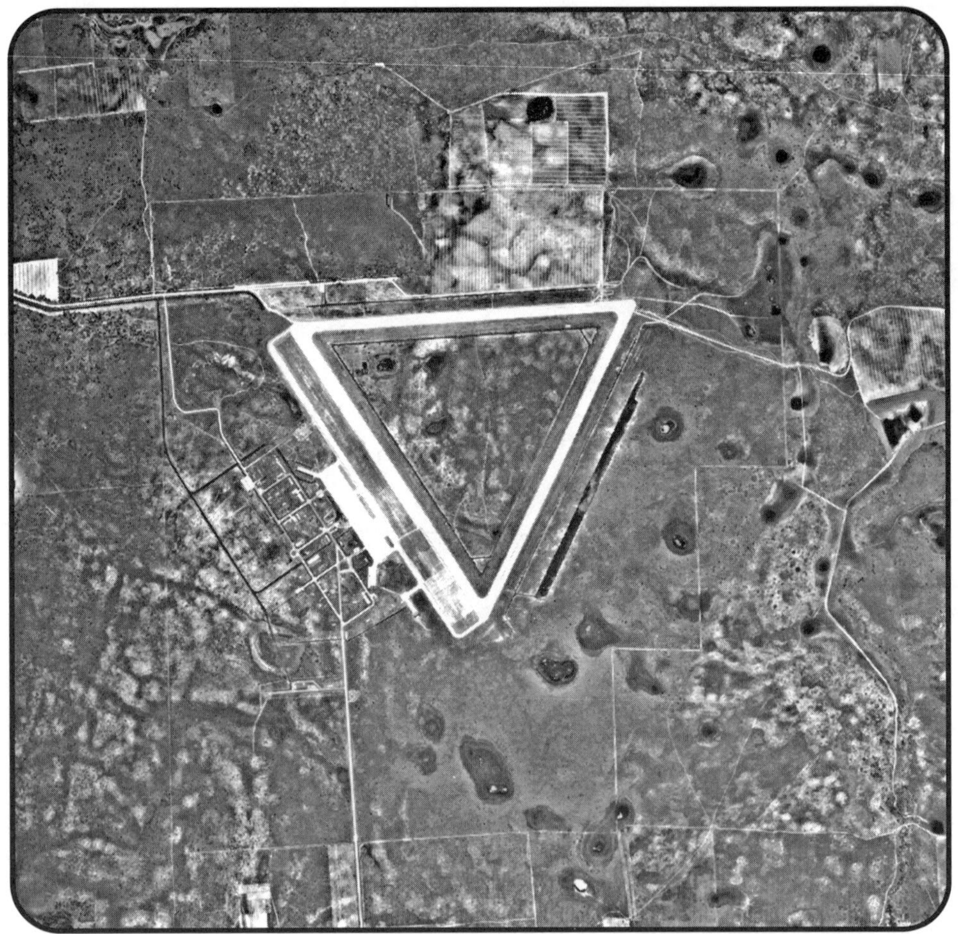

Photo: Punta Gorda Historical Society
Aerial View of Punta Gorda Army Airfield

On March 28, 1942, the 97th Bombardment Group (Heavy) officially transferred from MacDill to Sarasota. Construction of various facilities were not complete when the new group arrived, making living conditions nearly impossible. Flying the heavy B-17s the 97th carefully put wheels onto the new and untested runways, while the base engineers squirmed. The heavy B-17s landed easily on the double-layered asphalt-cement runways.

The four bombardment squadrons in the 97th (the 340th, 341st 342nd and the 414th) all flew from Sarasota. The 322nd Air Base Group provided all necessary service units. For the greater Sarasota area, the presence of the Army Air Corps group was an economic boom. Restaurants, shopkeepers and apartments were completely occupied.

SARASOTA AAF, SARASOTA

By July 1, 1942 the Army and local county officials had arranged a lease making the Sarasota-Manatee County Municipal Airport an official Army air base. Workers and material were rushed to the airfield. The tent cantonment areas were to be constructed as quickly as possible to house the influx of the training personnel. The Army and the WPA had work crews laboring at different places about the airport.

Photo: Sarasota Historical Society
Typical P-40 flight line at Sarasota Army Airfield

The 92nd Bomb Group, similar in structure to the 97th, consisted of 2,525 officers and enlisted men, and arrived May 18, 1942. Sarasota AAF was a very busy air facility, which was to mean the almost complete destruction of the overused and weakening runways. The 92nd had been training at nearby MacDill Field prior to its transfer to Sarasota. It had been activated in March of 1942.

In June 1942, Sarasota was officially designated as a sub-base of MacDill Field. Because the runways at Sarasota were not suitable to accommodate the heavy bombers, such as the B-17s, it was decided sometime in June to move the 92nd Bombardment Group elsewhere. The 69th Fighter Squadron was transferred from Drew Field to Sarasota. The 49th flew the P-39 Aircobra.

After the end of the war the airfield became known as the Sarasota-Bradenton Inter-national Airport.

TYNDALL AAF, PANAMA CITY

This air base was constructed and quickly activated early in 1941. It was named in honor of Lt. Frank B. Tyndall who was killed in a plane crash July 1930 in North Carolina. Designated by the Army Air Corps as a target range in the same year, it was some time before the facility was to be used to capacity. Aircraft practiced shooting live ammunition at sleeve tow-targets following behind another aircraft, usually an AT-6 trainer.

Considerable experimentation was conducted by Capt. H. M. Myers, the Haas Armament Officer, as to the mixing of paint, inks, and paraffin in an attempt to produce a number of colors which would show up satisfactorily on the target sleeve to enable scores for gunners to be accurate. With the constantly changing colors of the target sleeves everyone was treated to an aerial color show. Tyndall had few heavy bombers. B-17s stationed at the field for

Photo: Sararsota Historical Society

Aerial view of Sarasota training air base

Photo: Smithsonian Institute

Tyndall Army Airfield at Panama City

the purpose of training turret gunners as the Army considered the base to be a B-24 facility. However, no B-24s were transferred to Tyndall for this purpose. Lacking suitable training bombers, Tyndall still managed to graduate 500 gunners per week.

The ranges at Tyndall and the other gunnery schools were located a great distance from the base proper. The ranges were therefore divided into a gunnery school ground range and an air-to-air firing area or range. This was not an integrated range system such as was achieved at the flexible gunnery school at Buckingham Field, Fort Myers.

The usual ground training school instruction was followed by aerial training, beginning with moving land targets towed over a set course by a jeep. Stationary targets were also employed. It was the reality of the moving target sleeve that provided the best gunnery experience. Later old P-40s and P-40Bs were added to train fighter pilots. As the war wore on, improvements in equipment and technique improved. Today Tyndall covers some 28,000 acres and provides realistic training in the use of updated weapon systems.

VENICE AAF, VENICE

Up until the summer of 1941 the land that was to become the Venice Army Airfield was covered with palmetto scrub, pine trees and rattlesnakes. Situated directly on the Gulf, Venice was a quiet typical Florida tourist town. It was Finn W. Casperson who interested the Army in locating an airfield in Venice. Originally the site was investigated with an eye toward an anti-aircraft firing and training center, as well as a Coast Guard Artillery School and Target Range. Neither of these plans ever developed.

The site was finally approved as an air base to

Photo: Venice Historical Society

Typical entrance to Army air base, with gatehouse

train 3rd echelon maintenance crews. The two existing airstrips were investigated, one a grassed runway and the other, located just east of Highway 41, where the Venice schools are presently located. Instead, the site of the present Venice Municipal Airport was selected.

What started out as a cantonment for some 900 men was soon increased to accommodate more than 4,000 personnel. Barracks, hangars, frame buildings and shops of every kind, a sewage system (still in use this date), two concrete runways and aprons were all rushed into construction. The site would occupy some 1,200 acres of land.

The primary purpose of the air base was to provide for the training of service groups and, as such, it was permanently occupied by the 27th Service Group. On December 14, 1942, the 80th Service Group was the first to arrive for training. A system of factory-staffed engine schools operated at Venice. Among them: the Rollison Engine School, Republic, Rolls-Royce and Pratt and

Photo: Venice Historical Society

US Army aviation training and repair base at Venice

Whitney. Eventually, in addition to the service schools, instruction in flight operations was given to each new group of trainee pilots. The 14th Service Group, composed of about 400 Chinese personnel was also trained at Venice and they used the P-40s.

Pilot trainees were also schooled in fighter gun tactics, spending many hours on the Venice target range, from south of Casperson Beaches to Boca Grande. Today the Venice Army Airfield exists as the Venice Municipal Airport.

Chapter Four

The Naval Air Stations

The U.S. Navy has a long and rich association with the Sunshine State of Florida. In 1826 the Navy constructed a base south of the city of Pensacola. The U.S. Army also established a presence by constructing Fort McRee, Fort Barancas and The Redoubt.

With the outbreak of the American Civil War, Florida's Confederate troops seized the two forts and the Navy abandoned the Navy Yard. Union troops continued to hold Fort Pickens, located on Santa Rosa Island, throughout the war. In 1862, the Navy Yard was reoccupied by Federal troops. It would go on to serve as a base for Admiral Farragut's fleet in the blockade of Mobile Bay.

Key West was garrisoned by Federal troops as early as 1831 by two companies of the U.S. 6th Infantry Regiment. A more permanent fortification was started in 1845 by the Corps of Engineers. Key West remained in Federal hands throughout the Civil War.

With World War I raging throughout Europe, the Navy sought the use of the Florida Keys, especially Key West. A seaplane air station was established and by September 1917, the first of the Curtiss N-9 seaplanes arrived. Key West's location as the country's southernmost Naval base made it invaluable as a year-round air training center. More than 500 pilots were to be trained at the Key West Naval Air Station. The end of World War II saw the Key West facility decommissioned, seeing only occasional use until the outbreak of World War II.

Beginning in 1938 the Navy had two aviation establishments — NAS Pensacola and the limited use of Key West. All this was about to rapidly change. The beginning of negotiations for the site of NAS Jacksonville were in progress, with an eye toward the use of existing municipal fields throughout Florida.

With Pensacola and its many auxiliary training fields capable of training some 800 to 1,000 student pilots each month, establishing more training fields at Pensacola was one solution. Locating and building more sites (wherever) became a priority and Florida offered year-round flying conditions as well as communities providing land to help secure their economic base. Altogether, the Navy constructed and trained personnel at 25 main air stations, utilizing almost an equal number of auxiliary or emergency airfields. Pensacola and Jacksonville dominated all Navy aviation training as well as having a carrier available for training purposes.

The Navy's system for designating airfields was:

NAS.... NAVY AIR STATION
NAAS.... NAVY AUXILIARY AIR STATION
NAF.... NAVY AIRFIELD
NAAF.... NAVY AUXILIARY AIRFIELD
OLF.... OUTLYING FIELDS

Photo: US Navy

Primary trainer, an N2S on the ramp at NAS Jacksonville

Some of these OLFs were just a single paved airstrip, whereas others had barracks, fuel re-supply, hangars and more important — lights.

Not only did Navy air bases vary in size and operation but a station might have as few as one squadron of 18 aircraft and men to service the planes. Bases such as NAS Jacksonville and NAS Pensacola, with their many training airfields and schools, had thousands of personnel stationed there.

The airfields constructed by the Army and the Navy were built in such haste that it was not long before they were plagued by a variety

Photo: Official US Navy Photograph

A training flight of TBMs over NAS Whiting Field

of problems, everything from soil erosion to runway deterioration, sewage missmanagement and the pesky mosquitoes. Many a pilot fought his way across a runway filled with ever-growing potholes only to be blinded by blowing dust.

A vast number of bases in Florida were constructed for pilot and operational training. With a few exceptions, the Navy built most of its primary training airfields based on a geometric design, enormous octagons with six to eight runways intersecting at the center, as well as huge circles, triangles, parallelograms, hexagons and multi-pointed stars. These multi-runway fields made it possible for pilots in training to land against the wind from any direction.

With the advent of the German U-boat sinking cargo ships just off the Florida coast, the Navy hurriedly built bases that could handle and maintain the lighter-than-aircraft — commonly called blimps. Facilities at Meacham Field in Key West, NAS Richmond and NAS Jacksonville became the homes of the slow but deadly submarine-hunting blimps. Blimps were also stationed at Isle of Pines, NAS Banana River and San Julian.

Additionally, the Navy constructed or developed other facilities such as the UDT School at Fort Pierce, the Anti-submarine School at Boca Chica, a V-12 Unit at the University of Miami, a radar school at Hollywood and Coast Guard air stations at St. Petersburg. By the middle of 1942 the Navy had invested heavily in the east coast of Florida, training thousands of Navy aviators and crews.

NAS BANANA RIVER, COCOA BEACH

The Banana River Naval Air Station was a 1,824-acre site situated on a narrow strip of coastal land just a few miles south of Cocoa Beach, between the Atlantic Ocean and a landlocked saltwater lagoon called the Banana River. Commissioned in October of 1940, the Navy utilized the facility as a seaplane base. Its primary purpose was to train pilots and crews in the PBM flying boat.

As a result of the attack on Pearl Harbor and the increase of German submarine activity, PBM crews were rotated into a daily submarine patrol. Early in 1942, a scouting squadron of Kingfishers was stationed at NAS Banana River, allowing the PBMs to return to training status.

The air base consisted of four large 4,000-foot asphalt runways with three runways intersecting at one end. In addition to the original seaplane base, with its run-up ramps, it also provided mooring facilities for a single blimp. This was utilized more than once by the anti-submarine blimps working in the general vicinity. These were usually based out of Richmond.

The Navy established an aerial photography school, a navigational school and a facility to experiment with blind-landing equipment. The Aviation Repair Depot also overhauled aircraft from NAS Daytona Beach, Melbourne, Vero Beach and the Coast Guard at St. Augustine. The air station complement of men reached some 390 officers, 2,500 enlisted men and an additional 600 civilian employees.

It is worth noting that one PRM flying boat on

Photo: Official US Navy Photograph

Naval Air Station at Banana River located at Cocoa Beach

a night navigation training flight failed to return and is often referred to when relating tales of the Bermuda Triangle. The aircraft sent to search for the missing PRM also disappeared. This was not an uncommon occurrence on either coast, especially from training facilities.

When the war ceased, NAS Banana River remained an active base but slowly completed its mission. In September 1947 it closed, but was transferred to the Air Force and today serves as the USAF Eastern Space and Missile Center, as Patrick AFB.

NAAS BRONSON, PENSACOLA

With war in Europe exploding across the world, NAS Pensacola needed to increase its training facilities. A site for an outlying training field was selected about 12 miles west of Pensacola. The Navy purchased 640 acres of land, cleared it and constructed an airfield. Known originally as Tarkiln Field, the airfield was used by primary trainers, usually the Navy's version of the Stearman N2S biplane. The bright yellow primary trainers from nearby Corry Field also used the field for training purposes.

In March of 1942, the Navy added an additional 260 acres and constructed a seaplane base on the Perdido Bay side of the airfield. It was commissioned as NAAS Bronson Field in November of 1942 and served as a dual-purpose airfield until the end of the war. The airfield was named in honor of LTjg. Clarence Bronson, an early naval aviator.

NAAS Bronson consisted of a large geometric design — a circular asphalt mat, crisscrossed by four 4,000-ft. runways that all intersected in the center. This unusual arrangement allowed trainee pilots to land from any direction against the wind. Barracks, hangars, seaplane ramps, service buildings and other required structures were built in 1942. Typical of World War II training airfields, two outlying fields were utilized by Bronson, both located in nearby Alabama, (Faircloth and Kaiser). These two grass strips were used as training and emergency airfields.

Bronson eventually transitioned to a primary training program using some 300 SNJs or Texans. In addition to training pilots, the seaplane program included a course in the handling of PBYs.

The airfield closed in late 1946 and remained an outlying field (OLF) for nearby Saufley Field. Most of the support buildings were torn down, leaving the hangars as storage buildings.

Photo: Official US Navy Photograph

NAAS Bronson Field near Pensacola

(NAAS) CECIL FIELD, DUVAL COUNTY

Located today at the edge of Jacksonville just off Route 51, eight miles east of Maxville, is NAAS Cecil Field. The Navy uses Cecil Field as a home to the F-18 Hornet jet fighters. In early 1941, the Navy needed more airfields to supplement the pilot training programs at NAS Jacksonville. 2,666 acres were selected, approximately 16 miles southwest of

Jacksonville, purchased and construction began immediately. Within six months all construction was complete and Cecil Field began basic flight training shortly thereafter.

Improvement of the 2,000-acre geometrically circular, asphalt landing field was upgraded by the addition of four asphalt 5,000-ft. runways. The facility was used for flight training of pilots and as a carrier qualification base. Unlike Army pilots, Navy pilots had to learn the difficult task of landing a warbird on the deck of a rolling carrier. Named for CDR. Henry Barton Cecil, who lost his life in a dirigible crash, NAAS Cecil Field was commissioned on February 2, 1942.

NAAS Cecil Field maintained a training program for fighter and dive bomber pilots. Using the standard Navy dive bomber, the Dauntless SBD, and eventually the SB2C Hell Divers, pilots practiced gunnery and bomb runs on nearby target ranges. Mill Cove (Doctor's Lake), Amelia City, Black Creek and the Chafe ranges, to name a few, served as dive bombing sites. Dive bombing proved a costly factor to pilots and air crews. In the early going a large number of planes crashed while diving on target. The problems were analyzed and finally corrected, and the number of crashes greatly reduced.

Whitehouse Field in Jacksonville served as an outlying airfield for NAAS Cecil Field and NAS Jacksonville. Switzerland Field, St. Mary's (Georgia) and other NAS Jacksonville OLFs served the dive bombers from Cecil Field. It was this concentration of Naval installations that made Jacksonville a great liberty town.

NAAS Cecil Field today serves the Navy as a jet fighter base.

NAAS CORRY FIELD, PENSACOLA

The history of Corry Field begins with the end of World War I when the Navy decided it needed an auxiliary field to NAS Pensacola. On a 250-acre site located in present day Pensacola, between 9th Avenue and Palafox Highway, the Navy constructed a small field with barracks and support buildings. Primary training of pilots was conducted there for five to six years.

The Navy accepted land from the Escambia County Commission and, on 500 acres approximately 3 miles north of NAS Pensacola, constructed a new and larger airfield. The name Corry Field was transferred to the new site and the old field became an outlying field called City Field. The Navy named both sites in honor of Lcdr. William M. Corry, a Medal of Honor Navy aviator.

Corry Field actually consisted of two different airfields, defined as East or West Field, consisting of three long asphalt surfaced runways, all intersecting at the center point. The longest runway, 4,200 ft. in length, served as a landing and takeoff strip for multi-engine aircraft as part of the Intermediate Training Command.

In 1932 the field was updated with surfaced runways, large hangars and support

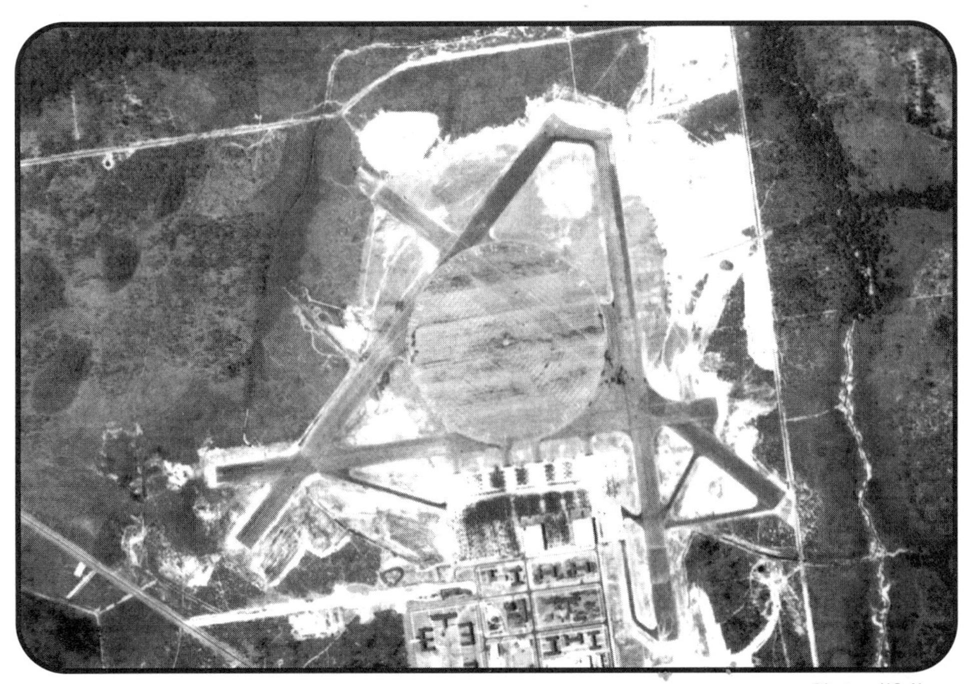

Photo: US Navy

NAAS Cecil Field, Jacksonville

Photo: US Navy

NAAS Corry Field near Pensacola

buildings. Prior to World War II, Corry Field served as a primary training field. Many Allied pilots received their primary training at Corry.

In addition to flying anti-submarine patrols from Corry, air-sea rescue and target tow planes also were stationed at the air base. By mid-1944 some 200 officers and 1,600 enlisted personnel were stationed at Corry, with 400 to 500 students. The special flight training school for Navy Flight Surgeons was also located at the field.

At the conclusion of the war Corry Field was reduced to a training facility for pilots of multi-engine aircraft. Today Corry Field serves as a naval technical training center, with schools for electronic warfare, instrumentation and cryptology. Many of the original pre-war buildings are still standing and used by the many schools.

NAS DAYTONA BEACH, DAYTONA BEACH

The Daytona Beach Municipal Airport consisted of two paved runways, a small hangar for light planes and an administration building. Planes normally shared the airfield with cattle that grazed alongside the runways. A commission led by Senator Claude Pepper and Congressman Joe Mendricks convinced the U.S. Navy that the airport would be an ideal site for flight training. The Navy awarded a contract for converting the airport and nearby golf course to a naval air station. A large flight hangar was erected, along with a control tower, classrooms, barracks and support buildings. Additional land was cleared, wetlands filled, a large drainage canal and four additional paved runways constructed. The site was commissioned on December 15, 1942 using the name of the city.

NAS Daytona Beach had four 4,000-ft. paved runways converging near one end. Four outlying fields were used — at Tonoka (Ormand Beach), Bunnell (some 24 miles northwest of Daytona Beach). New Symrna Beach (14 miles south) and Spruce Creek. The airfields at Bunnell and New Symrna Beach had control towers and barracks for a small cadre of personnel. Bunnell, known locally as Bulow Field, had four large 5,000-ft. runways and was considered at one time to be commissioned as an NAAS. New Symrna airfield contained a launch catapult and arresting gear set up for basic carrier training. Bunnell and New Symrna also contained facilities for gunnery training schools.

The first aircraft to use NAS Daytona Beach were the SNC-1 Falcons and the SBD-4 Dauntless dive bombers. In 1943 these aircraft were replaced by F4Fs, FM-I Wildcats and F6F Hellcats. Upon completion of their fighter training, these pilots went directly to the fleet for combat.

At capacity NAS Daytona Beach had 293 officers, 1,222 enlisted men with barracks available for 295 officers and 1,480 enlisted trainees. Additionally, an air-sea rescue crash boat facility was operat-

Photo. US Navy

NAS Daytona Beach training facility

ing from the New Symrna Yacht Club.

Today the airfield is the Daytona Beach Regional Airport. Adjacent to the airport is the Daytona International Speedway.

NAS DELAND, DELAND

In 1928 the airport at Deland consisted of a single runway and was privately owned. With the sense that aviation was growing, the city of Deland bought the facility in 1935 and established a municipal airport. Two 4,000-ft. asphalt paved runways, a hangar and an administration-control tower comprised the enterprise.

Following the course of other east coast communities, Deland offered the airport to the military. Accepting the offer, the Navy took a lease on the airport early in 1942. At the same time a third runway was being constructed by the CAA. Placing Deland under the direction of the Naval Operational Training Command, the Navy commissioned NAS Deland on November 17, 1942.

When the Navy took command of the municipal airport, a large hangar and other support biuldings were being constructed. During the war, the Navy added a fourth runway and extended the others to 6,000 feet. Larger administration buildings and barracks were constructed. By April of 1944, 331 officers and 1,140 enlisted personnel were stationed there. In

Photo: Deland Historical Society

The Lockheed Ventura crews were trained at NAS Deland.

addition to an assembly and maintenance facility, a boat facility was maintained on nearby Crescent Lake. It was assumed that if there were a choice, pilots would rather crashland on water than land. Spruce Creek airfield, southwest of NAS Daytona Beach, served as an OLF. Gunnery and bombing ranges at Mill Cove (Doctor's Lake) south of Orange Park, Black Creek and Amelia City were all used by NAS Deland.

The Lockheed Ventura, a twin-engine medium bomber, operated out of NAS Deland. During 1943 10 Ventura squadrons trained at Deland as well as the old standbys, Douglas SBD Dauntless dive bombers. Beginning in early 1944, the air base provided a course in Advanced Carrier Navigation for pilots. Hellcats replaced the SBDs in late 1944.

Deland closed in March 1946 and today is a thriving municipal airport and industrial park.

NAF DINNER KEY, DINNER KEY

The coastal island of Dinner Key is five miles south of populous Miami. It was named for a popular picnic site by pleasure boaters in the 1880s. It originally was a small strip of white sand but later was connected to the mainland by land-filling. With the U.S. Navy tied to seaplanes as the backbone of its air arm, Dinner Key was selected as a location to construct a seaplane base. In 1918 during World War I, the Navy commissioned the seaplane base as a Navy station. A dozen seaplanes and a few dirigibles conducted flight training for new aviators. At the end of World War I, the Navy Department closed the base and liquidated its properties. The sea plane facility was to continue in use by various commercial airlines, especially those that developed flying routes to South America.

The Coast Guard utilized the site in 1932 as an air station flying air-sea rescue aircraft. Pan American Airlines, still flying its world famous Pan American "flying boats," built a new terminal at the site. The U.S. Navy began using the facility again as early as 1942. The Navy finally took command of the site and commissioned it NAF Dinner Key in August 1943.

Pan American continued its presence at Dinner Key, conducting navigation ground school for training flights stationed there. The mission of NAF Dinner Key was to support the transport ferry planes which flew throughout southern Florida, the Caribbean and South America. In addition to the crash boat facility, PT boats used the station as a training base. Four large hangars, a large administration building and a control tower along with the seaplane ramps dominated the relatively small Naval Air Facility. Station personnel averaged 130 officers and 600 enlisted men with quarters to house 650 trainees. With the end of the War, Miami purchased the Key in 1946. The Coast Guard continued at Dinner Key until 1965 when it moved its operations to Miami's Opa-Locka Field.

Photo: US Navy

NAF Dinner Key served as a seaplane base, five miles from the city of Miami.

NAAS ELLYSON, PENSACOLA

Photo: Official US Navy Photograph

NAAS Ellyson Field flight training near Pensacola

With a need to expand NAS Pensacola, the Navy acquired land one-half mile east of Route 90 and about 7 miles outside the city of Pensacola. Ellyson was originally developed with just two short 3,700-ft. runways. It was called Base Field by those who were stationed there. It was opened for operations as a training field in February 1941. Later in the year, as is Navy tradition, the base was commissioned OLF Ellyson Field, in honor of CRD. Theodore Ellyson, the first Navy aviator.

Ellyson had two major airfields known as East Field and West Field. Each field had six additional asphalt paved runways. There was a single large hangar and one repair unit. All this changed when the Japanese bombed Pearl Harbor. Administrative control was located at NAS Pensacola until January 1, 1943, when it was commissioned NAAS Ellyson. Three OLFs were assigned to Ellyson — OLF Baghdad, OLF Spencer and OLF Canal (near Foley, Alabama).

OLF Baghdad was located approximately 12 miles northeast of Ellyson, a mile or so south of Milton. It had one of those wonderful geometric designs, an 8-pointed star with 8,100-ft. asphalt paved runways. OLF Spencer, located in the town of Pace and OLF Canal all had similar runway designs.

Ellyson's mission was to train Navy aviators in the use of the Vultee SNV Valiant, a most difficult aircraft. It was known as the "Vultee Vibrator," due to its two-stage propeller and its constant irritating vibration. The SNV was a trainer used to train pilots in the intermediate courses. Both the Vultee SNV and the SNJ were utilized as training aircraft at Ellyson. The SNJ was better suited to the fixed gunnery instruction and eventually replaced all the SNVs by war's end.

The base consisted of 180 officers and 1,350 enlisted personnel with space available for about 700 students. When the war ended, NAAS Ellyson was used for storage of aircraft from Pensacola. Today it has been passed on for civilian use as an industrial park.

NAS FORT LAUDERDALE, FORT LAUDERDALE

With German submarines prowling the coastal waters and attacking Allied shipping close to Florida, the citizens of Fort Lauderdale organized to protect themselves. The nearby Coast Guard Auxiliary and Civil Air Patrol maintained a lookout for submarines. Fort Lauderdale felt somewhat secure with the Coast Guard facility (Base Six) on the present site of Bahia Mar.

Port Everglades, with its fueling and repair facility, readily lent itself to use by the Navy. By June 1942, the Navy had taken over the Merle L. Fogg airfield, acquired nearby land and commenced to enlarge the airport. The Fort Lauderdale Municipal Airport was begun in 1926. The CAA made improvements until the war began. Named for the city, NAS Fort Lauderdale was commissioned October 1, 1942. It was placed under the Naval Air Operational Training Command.

NAS Fort Lauderdale consisted of four 5,000-ft. asphalt paved runways intersecting at a center point. The station had two OLFs — at North Pompano, some 30 miles north, and West Prospect at Oakland Park. NAS Fort Lauderdale maintained a grass strip as an emergency field just west of Davie. With a single large repair hangar, the Naval Air Station with its warm sunny weather was dubbed an outdoor facility.

The station's primary mission was the training of pilots and crewmen for Grumman TBF and TBM torpedo bombers. Pilots and aircrews turned over every 6-8 weeks. Training consisted of dropping torpedoes at moving targets and shooting at tow target sleeves. On North Beach .50 caliber machine guns were used by crewmen for target practice and teaching. Ensign George Bush attended NAS Fort Lauderdale as a pilot trainee.

Today the former Naval Air Station has reverted to civilian use and has become the Fort Lauderdale-Hollywood International Airport.

Photo: Fort Lauderdale Historical Society

NAS Fort Lauderdale fighter training facility

USNATB FORT PIERCE, FORT PIERCE

The United States Naval Amphibious Training Base at Fort Pierce opened on January 26, 1943 under the command of Capt. Clarence Gulbranson. The Second World War first most dramatically affected the city of Fort Pierce via German submarine sinkings allied of shipping offshore. Rescued survivors were pulled from the sea and brought to Fort Pierce for treatment and hospitalization. Fort Pierce helped in rescue efforts of numerous sinkings.

As with other communities in Florida realizing their extraordinary location on the coast, Fort Pierce petitioned and lobbied the Federal Government to locate a training facility there. It appeared that the military ignored the community as one after another locations were utilized by the Army or Navy, except Fort Pierce.

Events in the South Pacific and the possible invasion of Europe would soon impact Fort Pierce. The experience of the U.S. Forces in Operation Torch, the amphibious invasion of North Africa, was not to be forgotten. A site was to be selected where consistent good weather and suitable beaches could be used to train crews in amphibious landings in small craft carrying Army combat engineers, beach battalions, Navy Seabees, scouts and raiders, and the underwater demolitions teams.

With Fort Pierce located on the east coast of Florida it was protected from the poundings of the Atlantic Ocean by Hutchinson Island. It was an ideal site for amphibious related training. The Burston Hotel, formerly a small tourist hotel, was used for as much lodging and support as it could provide. A

Photo: US Navy

Amphibious practice landings in small craft at Fort Pierce

tent city was constructed directly on the beach, and as one former sailor remarked, "You went to sleep at night with the surf sounding in your ears."

The training of young sailors and some soldiers in the proper handling of landing craft or so-called "Attack Boats" was important. The forthcoming invasion of Europe at Normandy would demand not only skill but also nerve, and Fort Pierce would produce that valuable kind of training. After becoming familiar with the many types of invasion craft, crewmen were instructed in basic boat handling in the calm waters of the wide Indian River lagoon. Following much practice of putting a boat "square" onto the beach, crews took their small boats out to sea to practice landings in the high Atlantic surf. These crews took their craft onto the beaches over and over again with and without troops on board, under combat conditions until each of the four-man crew members became skilled in each other's assignments. Physical conditioning was a watchword of the program, as was constant training in small arms.

Tied closely to an invasion with small craft is the proper training of shore parties. The military personnel who attempted to organize and bring order to the massive confusion of boats, landing ships and troops are the beach battalions, the so-called shore parties. Because of the necessity of putting Army troops onto the beaches, beach battalion training became a joint venture utilizing the Army combat engineers and the Navy. The training was concentrated and highly specialized. It was repetitive training, until all hands could "do it in their sleep." Billeted at Fort Pierce was a SEABEE unit that constructed on North Beach replicas of obstacles planted on the Normandy beaches by the German Army. All types of devices that were anticipated to be encountered by underwater demolition teams were built for live training.

The scouts and raiders trained at USNATB Fort Pierce compiled distinguished records for heroism and action in the Mediterranean, Europe, India,

Photo: US Navy

USNATB at Fort Pierce used to train amphibious crews, Army engineers, beach battalions and UDT Crews

Burma and China.

Because of the disastrous results of the Marine invasion of Tarawa in the Pacific, the Navy decided to begin training underwater demolition teams. Lcdr. Draper R. Kauffman was placed in charge of the new units. The training unit at Fort Pierce became the home for the UDT during World War II.

USNATB Fort Pierce was officially decommissioned on February 2, 1946 but will always remain in the hearts of the residents there. Today a museum is located on North Hutchinson Island preserving the history of the U.S. Navy UDT.

NAAS GREEN COVE SPRINGS, GREEN COVE SPRINGS

The small city of Green Cove Springs is located on the west bank of the wide St. Johns River. In 1939 it had an excellent municipal airport that caught the eye of the U.S. Navy as it sought to develop NAS Jacksonville. After securing a lease on the airport, construction quickly began in August. The station opened in March 1941 as an auxiliary field. Named Lee Field, for Ens. Benjamin Lee, it was utilized as a primary training facility. Lee Field remained under the administrative command of NAS Jacksonville.

Lee Field contained four 5,000-ft. asphalt paved runways, called the "A" type runways by pilots. Two large hangars were constructed, as were barracks for 600 officers and 2,000 enlisted personnel. The commissioning of NAAS Green Cove Springs occurred on February 20, 1943. OLFs were located at St. Augustine, Switzerland and Fleming Island. Gunnery target range flights were conducted from Palatka to the south.

In the beginning of primary training, cadets utilized the familiar N2S Stearmans and NR-1 Ryan Recruits. Later SNJs were incorporated. In 1943, after many changes in aircraft training, the Navy removed them and stationed Operational Training Units using the Grumman Wildcat and the Corsair. In addition to the usual aircraft check-out, carrier qualifications were conducted.

Gunnery and bombing flights utilized Mill Cove, Amelia City, Black Creek and the Chafe ranges as well as the gunnery range at Palatka. These pilots were being trained to provide ground support for troops involved in the difficult battles on the islands of the Pacific.

Today the former Navy air base serves as the Clay County Port alongside the St. Johns River. A single runway survives from the original base, and it is used as a private airstrip.

Photo: US Navy

NAAS Green Cove Springs flight and gunnery training facility near Jacksonville NAS

Photo: US Navy

air bases in 1938. Of five sites local to Jacksonville, the Board decided on Camp Foster. Since a carrier was to be part of the training program, Jacksonville's Camp Foster was selected. Jacksonville approved a $1.1 million bond issue to buy the needed land and for a naval base at Mayport to house the carriers. The Army transferred its base at Camp Foster, buildings and all, to Camp Blanding and the Navy moved in. Construction began immediately, clearing land for runways, hangars, barracks and support buildings. NAS Jacksonville was officially commissioned on October 15, 1940.

LEFT: Gunnery training school located at NAS Jacksonville

BELOW: Aerial view of NAS Jacksonville

Photo: US Navy

NAS JACKSONVILLE, JACKSONVILLE

The site of NAS Jacksonville at Black Point was originally an Army base during World War I, known as Camp Johnson. Through out the 1920s and 1930s the site was called Camp Foster and served as a National Guard training camp.

As a result of the six-member Hepburn Board, the Navy was to build three major

Designed to be an operational training and repair base, NAS Jacksonville, or JAX as it was commonly known, served as a primary training station. It had four 6,000-ft. asphalt paved runways, five large hangars, a major repair building and a maintenance facility. The seaplane facility housed two seaplane hangars, barracks and support buildings. A large Naval Hospital, the Naval Air Technical Training Center, radio control tower, parachute rigger's loft and crash boat facilities were quickly added to the main base.

Photo: US Navy

Anti-submarine aircraft training facility, NAS Key West

Jacksonville's Municipal Airport, then utilized by the Army as an anti-submarine base, was acquired and placed under the administration of NAS Jacksonville. It was commissioned in April 1944 as NAAS Jacksonville Municipal #1, Florida. NAAS Cecil Field, Green Cove Springs and Mayport served as auxiliary airfields to NAS Jacksonville. Altogether the air stations in the Jacksonville command utilized 12 OLFs.

Today NAS Jacksonville airfield is known as Towers Field in honor of Admiral John H. Towers.

NAS KEY WEST, KEY WEST

Key West, known as the "Gibraltar of the Gulf" during the American Civil War, has been a Navy base since 1823. It remained in Union hands throughout the Civil War, protected by the Federal Navy. In the war with Spain, it was again used as a fleet staging base against Cuba.

Ground was broken for construction of a small air patrol station in July 1917. It involved considerable dredging and fills in order to accommodate a dirigible hangar, seaplane ramps, various station and support buildings and barracks. The facility was used as a primary pilot training base and was used for anti-submarine patrols. When World War I ended, only occasional use was made of the base until the advent of World War II.

Beginning in 1939 a major expansion of the air station occurred, adding airfields on Boca Chica Key and Meacham Field for increased use of lighter-than-aircraft. Meacham also served as an OLF to Boca Chica. At the time of the Japanese attack on Pearl Harbor, there were three main facilities at Key West — OLF Meacham Field, NAAS Boca Chica and a seaplane base located at Trumbo Point.

It was the Army that actually built the asphalt paved runways at Meacham Field. The Army quickly withdrew leaving the coastal duties to the Navy. The Navy added two additional runways and maintained a blimp airfield.

The Army improved Boca Chica and used it for anti-submarine purposes. In 1943 the Army turned the airfield over to the Navy who in turn used it as an air station for the training of land and carrier based aircraft in anti-submarine warfare. A 10,000-ft. airstrip located at Marathon Key served as an OLF for Boca Chica. In 1945 the entire operation was consolidated as NAS Key West. NAS Key West would once again become the center of national attention in 1962 with the military confrontation of the Cuban missle crisis.

NAS LAKE CITY, LAKE CITY

Lake City, located in northcentral Florida, had a small, 2-runway airport in 1938. Located just east of the city, the airfield was utilized primarily by owners of private airplanes. As with other communities, in 1941 Lake City negotiated with the military to lease the field. The Navy accepted, as it was reasonably close to NAS Jacksonville and NAAS Cecil Field.

Construction began on May 1942, building three 6,000-ft. runways and one 7,000-ft. asphalt paved runway. Three runways formed a giant letter "A" with the vertical center runway. A single large service repair hangar was constructed along with barracks, support buildings and ammunition storage bunkers. An OLF was located about 20 miles southeast on the outskirts of the town of Lake Butler. Navigational flights were made to Lake Butler as well as to auxiliary fields at Cedar key, Alachua and Stengel fields in Gainesville.

NAS Lake City utilized the Lockheed twin-engine PV-1 Ventura to train instructors of multi-engine aircraft. Although originally designed as a medium bomber, the Ventura served as a highly effective weapon against German submarines. The station training cadre had a complement of 290 officers and 1,150 enlisted personnel. During 1943 and until the end of the war, about 200 WAVES were stationed at NAS Lake City and served in a variety of capacities. Many served in the administration offices, meteorological services and in aircraft repair. In addition to training personnel, the base maintained a large repair and assembly section. Because of this and the unusually long runways, it was utilized as a repair stop for the heavy bombers of the Ferry Transport Command.

Today NAS Lake City is the home of Lake City Community College and a private facility, Aero Corporation.

Photo: Lake City Historical Society

Lockheed PV-1 training facility at NAS Lake City

NAAS MAYPORT, MAYPORT

Situated at the coastal mouth of the St. Johns River, the small town of Mayport was originally developed as a major naval base to accommodate one or more aircraft carriers to provide carrier training for NAS Jacksonville pilots. A site was selected by the Navy at Bibault Bay to serve as a carrier port complex with an adjoining airfield. Initial dredging at Ribault Bay began in early 1940, but was not completed until 1941. The dredge spoil was utilized to construct a nearby airfield. Planes could be lifted from a carrier deck by large cranes and then placed on a paved ramp that led directly to the airfield.

NAAS Mayport consisted of 700 acres. It had four asphalt paved runways that formed a most intricate geometric pattern. The shortest runway was about 4,000 ft., and the longest was 4,500 ft. As part of the main base docking facility, the air station had barracks for 50 officers and 250 enlisted personnel. As WAVES graduated from NAS Jacksonville training schools, some 50 were stationed at NAAS Mayport. NAAS Mayport was officially commissioned on March 20, 1943.

The primary mission of NAAS Mayport was to refuel and rearm fighter aircraft that landed there from other air bases. Light main-

Photo: US Navy

NAAS Mayport utilized as a rearm and refuel facility

tenance was provided if it could be handled within a single day. Initially a Navy air facility, Mayport later became an NAAS but was utilized more as an OLF to Jacksonville.

The aircraft carrier stationed at Mayport Naval Base served as an instructional moving platform for pilots training to take off and land on a moving carrier deck. The base also maintained several crash boats and Kingfisher float planes for air-sea rescue purposes. At one point during 1943, a torpedo squadron utilized the base as a training facility. Squadrons of PT boats used the base as operational training. The Coast Guard maintained a beach patrol facility at Mayport to guard against German boat landings. Today Mayport remains a naval base, serving the nuclear carrier fleet.

NAS MELBOURNE, MELBOURNE

Melbourne today serves as the hub of what in Brevard County is commonly called the "Space Coast of America." Located overlooking the Indian River, Melbourne faces eastward toward the Atlantic, across the very southern tip of Merritt Island.

Seeking to profit from the lucrative air mail contracts, the city developed as an airfield a site northwest and away from populated areas. It was to serve as a refueling and light maintenance facility. Utilizing WPA funds, the city moved the airport to its present position. The Navy took over the facility in October 1942 and immediately set about enlarging the airfield. A single large hangar was built, with barracks, support facilities and assorted small-caliber gun

Photo: US Navy

Aerial gunnery training facility at NAS Melbourne

ranges.

Melbourne had four 4,000-ft. asphalt paved runways that converged at the Indian River end of the airfield. Quarters were maintained for some 370 officers and 1,200 enlisted personnel. A major repair and assembly facility was also located at Melbourne to service the training cadre's aircraft. WAVES were stationed here after 1943. Early in 1945, 300 German POWs were billeted in a compound. They worked in the laundry and mess facilities.

Utilizing F4F Wildcats and F6F Hellcats, pilots were trained in gunnery procedures for fighter planes. Because of the long stretch of unpopulated coastline, the gunnery school used aircraft with a tow target sleeve.

At the OLF Valkaria, located 2fi miles south of Malabar, a small airfield also served as a training station. This field was equipped with a catapult and landing arresting gear to train pilots for carrier landings, and was used for familiarization flights to and from Melbourne.

NAS Melbourne was closed in February 1945 and returned to the city of Melbourne, and today is the Melbourne International Airport.

NAS MIAMI, MIAMI

At the end of World War I the Navy dismantled the dirigible hangar at Key West and brought it to Opa Locka outside Miami. The Navy established a Naval Reserve Training Base at Opa Locka. With the approach of war in Europe, the Navy began construction to convert the facility into a major air base. The Opa Locka field remained as part of a larger air station known as NAS Miami.

While Opa Locka conducted basic primary flight training, NAS Miami conducted Phase 2 or intermediate training. NAS Miami consisted of three separate air fields: Opa Locka, Miami Municipal Airport and Master Field. Opa Locka consisted of two separate airfields, East Field and West Field, joined by a taxiway. Each field had four asphalt paved runways, the longest 3,700 ft. and the shortest 2,300 ft. NAS Miami and Master Field each had four asphalt paved runways, hangars, barracks and support buildings.

At its peak, the complex known as NAS Miami housed 700 officers and 7,200 enlisted personnel. By the end of 1943 about 200 WAVES also were stationed there. NAS Miami housed a Naval Air Gunnery School, at which WAVES often served as gunnery instructors. The station also maintained a large repair section which serviced the base aircraft as well as Ferry Transport Command planes on demand.

At the beginning or the war, NAS Miami conducted fighter and dive bomber training. Eventually torpedo training units #2 and #63 were transferred from NAS Jacksonville. At the peak of training the number of aircraft reached about 600 on station. To service this number of planes, auxiliary airfields at North Ferry, South Ferry, Forman, Davie and Richmond served as OLFs to NAS Miami. North and South Ferry Fields were U.S. Army facilities that were also used by the Navy. Forman also served as an OLF to NAS Fort Lauderdale. In addition to NAS Miami, the Navy also conducted several tech-

Photo: US Navy

Fighter and dive bomber training facility at NAS Miami

nical training schools. NAS Miami was returned to civilian use in 1947, and Reserve personnel used Master Field.

NAS PENSACOLA, PENSACOLA

On December 17, 1917, the Naval Aeronautic Station at the Pensacola Navy Base was redesigned as Naval Air Station Pensacola. With the declaration of war on April 19, 1917, the expansion of the facility went forward. The demands for skilled Navy pilots, crews and support units were enormous. Radio, photography, navigation and bombing schools were hurriedly assembled. During the war the mission of naval aviation was to protect our coastal areas from German submarines.

The base was demobilized when international agreements restricted the growth of naval aviation. During the 1920s, in a move to utilize aircraft other than seaplanes, NAS Pensacola's Station Field, the blimp and dirigible field, was enlarged, and in 1936 was renamed Chevalier Field. It was named for LCDR. Godfrey Chevalier, who made the first landing on an aircraft carrier deck.

Beginning in 1938, NAS Pensacola added and enlarged facilities with an eye toward war. The Navy base was restructured to berth a carrier to be utilized in pilot training. With the advent of the war, NAS Pensacola was training 2,500 student pilots each month. A variety of training facilities were located at Pensacola — seaplane operations with scout and observation instruction, Naval Air Surgeons Training, flexible gunnery, Naval Air Photography and a large school facility for Aviation Maintenance.

Twenty-nine airfields served the frantic pace of training and were identified as Naval Auxiliary Air Stations, Outlying Fields or day emergency fields.

Many Allied pilots from England, France and a scattering of Canadians received their flight training at many of the auxiliary fields. Today NAS Pensacola maintains a privately funded, outstanding Naval Air Museum. Headquarters for Naval Air Basic Training Command is still located at Pensacola, and the roar of training jets reminds residents of the living history of its Naval Air Station.

NAS RICHMOND, RICHMOND

Early 1940 found German submarine activity getting closer to the eastern coast of the United States. The need for anti-submarine warfare by aircraft became apparent. The blimp facility at NAS Key West had been enlarged, but the need for submarine detection in waters surrounding Miami became painfully obvious.

Official US Navy Photograph

Primary aviation training station for the US Navy at NAS Pensacola

A site of about 2,100 acres was selected 15 miles southwest of Miami. Early in 1941 construction on a large lighter-than-aircraft hangar began. NAS Richmond was officially commissioned on September 1942. Shortly thereafter Blimp Patrol Squadron ZP-21 arrived. ZP-21 was comprised of the K model (or size) blimp which, of the four sizes used during the war, ranked 3rd largest. ZP-21 was a large blimp squadron with some fifteen K-sized airships. Many of these were deployed to other blimp detachments at Key

Photo: US Navy

Coastal blimp patrol station at NAS Richmond

West, San Julian, Banana River and Isle of Ines (in South Carolina). In addition to engaging German submarines at sea, the blimps served a valuable role, especially during the height of submarine activity in 1942-1943, in rescuing the survivors of U-boat sinkings. A coordinated effort between blimps and the Coast Guard saved many survivors.

NAS Richmond, named after its location, Richmond Heights, was constructed with three 1,000-ft. hangars designed to store more than one blimp. It also had barracks and blimp support buildings. A helium plant facility and a Helium Operators School were also located here. The station had two standard aircraft runways that crossed the enormous 2,000-ft. asphalt pave field mat. Richmond contained 8 mooring circles to hold blimps. About 100 officers and 600 enlisted personnel were stationed at the facility. It was not a training base. Blimps stationed at NAS Richmond patrolled the coastal beaches and offshore waters.

On September 13, 1945, a hurricane tore through the greater Miami area and the Navy, believing in the durability of the three large hangars, filled them with as many local aircraft as possible. Downed electrical lines ignited and destroyed all three hangars with a total loss of aircraft and 25 blimps. Richmond soon after closed in 1945. The property now belongs to the public domain.

NAS SANFORD, SANFORD

The Lockheed PV-1 Ventura was an excellent aircraft used in anti-submarine warfare. It was capable of carrying standard iron bombs or depth charges. With the U. S. Army slowly relinquishing protection of the waters offshore to the Navy, PV-1 Ventura facilities were hurriedly located along the east coast of Florida. The Navy selected a site located 2 1/2 miles south of Sanford. The city arranged to deed the Navy 1,490 acres for an Air Station.

Photo: US Navy

Ventura twin-engined training facility at NAS Sanford

Construction of a large hangar, barracks, administration building and support facilities began immediately. NAS Sanford was officially commissioned on November 3, 1942.

The station consisted of four 6,000-ft. asphalt runways that formed an enormous cross. About 360 officers and 1,400 enlisted personnel were stationed there during the war. 150 WAVES were also stationed at NAS Sanford from 1943 to 1945. A Repair Detachment overhauled and maintained the unit's aircraft.

NAS Sanford's mission was to check out pilots in the handling and flying of the Venturas. This involved making checkout flights to outlying fields such as OLF Osceola and Titusville-Cocoa. In addition to navigational flights, gunnery and bombing skills were honed either at over-water targets in the Atlantic or at one of the ranges maintained at NAS Jacksonville. Upon demand, flights of Venturas were utilized in search-and-destroy missions against German subs between Key West and the Jacksonville area. This often entailed searching for survivors.

The Sanford Municipal airport west of town was upgraded and used as an emergency field during the war, especially when the Venturas were replaced by the FM-1 Wildcat. The Grumman F6F Hellcat was added to the training mix and NAS Sanford became a Navy fighter training facility.

NAS Sanford was decommissioned in 1946 and returned to the city of Sanford. With the advent of the Korean War in 1950, NAS Sanford was re-established and served as a fighter training facility. Today the facility is the Sanford Municipal Airport.

NAS VERO BEACH, VERO BEACH

Today Vero Beach is home of the Piper Aircraft Corporation. During World War II it provided a unique function in Navy aviation, serving as a night fighter training base. Vero Beach had constructed a small municipal airport located one mile northwest of the city. It had a paved airfield and was used by Eastern Airlines as a refueling and light maintenance facility. With an eye to the war in Europe and Asia, the CAA allocated funds to upgrade the airport. At the beginning of the war, both the Army and the Navy scrambled to obtain the Vero Beach airport. In accordance with the Stratemeyer-Towers Line policy, the Navy leased the airport and acquired an additional 500 acres of land.

Construction began immediately, creating a total of six asphalt paved landing strips, one of which was 6,000 ft. in length, and barracks for 300 officers and 1,700 enlisted personnel, and a large hangar and other support buildings. The Beachland Hotel, the Sebastian Inn and several large apartment houses were utilized to house base personnel. NAS Vero Beach was commissioned November 1942 and remained as part of the Naval Air Operational Training Command.

NAS Vero Beach had a mission as a fighter training facility. Two separate fighter-training units were assigned fighter training status. Training Unit VF#1 taught skills in night fighting. The Grumman F6F Hellcat and Brewster SB2A Buccaneers served as training aircraft, with the F6F Hellcat being modified for night fighter training. Radar, especially redesigned for fighter aircraft, was placed under the wing in a pod to aid navigation at night. These night training flights took pilots to many outlying airfields equipped for night landings (and to some that were not, such as OLF Fort Pierce, Stuart, Sebastian and Roseland). Not an easy exercise to master, there were several pilots who were lost during the night instruction. Some were never located.

A crash boat, air-sea rescue facility was operated out of Fort Pierce to search for downed pilots. NAS Vero Beach today is the Municipal Airport and serves several commuter airlines.

Photo: US Navy

Combat fighter training facility at NAS Vero Beach

Chapter Five

The Air Schools

In 1939 the lights in Europe were suddenly shut off by the German war machine. At the time all U.S. Army flight training was done at Randolph Field in San Antonio, Texas. The Army was trying to quietly ready itself for war. The Army Air Corps realized that aircraft production could well outstrip the pilot training program. Randolph Field was only graduating 500 pilots per year!

Hap Arnold, General of the Army Air Corps, realized that to construct another training facility such as Randolph Field would take another four to five years. There was no possible way he could obtain the number of qualified aviators the country would soon need. He then turned to a group of friends who were operating their own commercial flying schools located throughout the United States. Would they help in training pilots for the Army? The answer was an unqualified yes!

Pilot cadets were typically young civilians from all over the United States. All went directly into cadet flight training. This primary training was conducted at airfields operated by civilian air schools. Each cadet typically went through 9 to 10 weeks of ground instruction along with 60+ hours of flight training. The Stearman PT-13 biplane was the most commonly used trainer. Upon completion of primary training, a cadet entered basic training, during which time the cadet flew the famed Vultee BT-13. basic training and advanced training took place at Army Air Corps bases generally located in Florida.

Photo: Arcadia Historical Society

Student pilots on the training flight line at Carlstrom Field, Arcadia

Seven private aviation colleges or schools were located in Florida. These were the Greenville Aviation School at Ocala (operated by Frank A. Hanley); the Lodwick Schools at Lakeland and Avon Park (owned by Albert I. Lodwick); the Riddle-McKay Aero College at Clewiston; the Embry-Riddle Schools at Dorr and Carlstrom fields in Arcadia; and air colleges were also located at Orlando and Miami.

At first the Army Air Corps sent small groups of cadets to these schools, as did the Allies. By 1944 the system worked so well, the schools were turning out 110,000 qualified pilots a year. As a response to the ever-increasing demand, the operators enlarged their facilities and built new schools. The civilian schools came under the command and supervision of the Army. Despite Army control, cadets were taught by civilian pilot instructors.

The schools offered basic pilot qualification training. The new pilots would then go to advanced pilot training or Army aviation schools. From intermediate training, some pilots would proceed to fighter pilot schools, bomber schools or the Ferry Transport Command. Altogether 62 civilian schools throughout the nation trained military pilots.

Typical of the operation were the Embry-Riddle schools at Carlstrom and Dorr fields in Arcadia. Carlstrom Field was originally built to train pilots for World War I. At that time, the Jenny biplane was used for pilot training. The airfield was officially closed in 1922, there being no need for additional military pilots. It was reopened and enlarged by March 1941 for pilot training. Instead of the Jenny trainer, the Stearman biplane was used there.

Carlstrom, now operated by Embry-Riddle, was larger, and equipped with suitable barracks, modern support building and improved airstrips. The ground school building contained six large classrooms and one that housed the Link Trainers. Carlstrom provided pilots 25 hours of night and instrument flying. Six large hangars were located on a wide curved flight line.

Photo: Arcadia Historical Society

Stearman flight trainers at Carlstrom Field

Dorr field was located on flatlands east of Arcadia, about seven miles from Carlstrom. Dorr had also been used as a pilot training school during World War I, but was in disrepair. In 1942 John Riddle took it over and completely rebuilt it. Dorr was one of four aviation schools operated by Riddle, three of which were in Florida.

The Dorr Field complex was named for Private Dorr, who died in a flying accident in Canada in 1917. Barracks at the field were very different from other military standards, being Colonial in design. Carlstrom and Dorr fields utilized the Stearman PT-17 biplane as their primary trainer for both American and Allied pilot training. Carlstrom and Dorr fields closed at the end of the war, with the distinction and record of having trained over 7,500 cadets with only a single fatality. A remarkable achievement! Cadets there flew a total of 650,000 hours.

Lodwick Aviation at Avon Park occupied a large winter resort hotel at the edge of Lake Lillian. Albert I. Lodwick, long a well-known local figure in early aviation, obtained the use of the hotel and had it converted to cadet quarters. It was spacious, with a large dining room that served as the facilities mess hall. Eventually in 1942, as the number of cadets increased, the typical Army-style wooden barracks were added. The ground school was situated in the old golf clubhouse.

The Lodwick School of Aeronautics located at Lakeland was also owned and operated by Albert I. Lodwick. The original operation had been located at Lincoln, Nebraska, but on August 1940 it was moved to Lakeland. Nine civilian flying instructors and nine civilian mechanics operated the civilian end of the training program. Lodwick bought the school, changed the name from the Lincoln School of Aeronautics to the Lodwick School of Aeronautics and continued training Army cadet pilots.

The school was located at the edge of the Lakeland Municipal Airport which was leased to the school. Students were housed at the Thelma Hotel until barracks were constructed. 300 or more student cadets were training at Lakeland at any one time. From June 1941 to October 1942, British and other Allied cadets were trained alongside American cadets.

Unlike many of the temporary Army Air Corps training fields made of asphalt paved runways, concrete runways crisscrossed the Lakeland Airport. There were no fewer than five auxiliary airfields that served the busy training field — the Halder-Elder Field at Eaton Park, Lake Wales Airfield, Winter Haven Airfield, Coronet Field at Plant City and Zephryhills.

Riddle-McKay built a $2 million facility at Clewiston near Lake Okeechobee. The school was opened in 1941 and primary training began for RAF cadets. As with Lakeland, American and other Allied pilots were trained at the same time. By the end of the war about 2,500 British Royal Air Force and other Allied pilots had been trained at the Clewiston facility. With the need for fighter pilots,

Photo: Smithsonian Institute

Aerial view of Carlstrom training field

Allied pilots were then sent to Army bases located throughout Florida for intermediate and fighter training. Others were sent to heavy bomber schools or to the Ferry Transport Command. All cadet pilots spent time in Link Trainers, putting in hours of night flying and long distance cross-country navigational flights. They also spent time at the Everglades and other gunnery ranges, honing their gunnery skills.

The Greenville Aviation School at Ocala originally started out of Greenville, Mississippi. Frank Hanely changed the location of the school to Ocala, but retained the school's name. Taylor Field, located southwest of the town, was hurriedly expanded and was ready in five weeks to receive the first class of cadets in November 1941.

The base had three 4,000-ft. runways, the usual wooden two-story barracks, ground school, hangars, maintenance support shops, as well as many other support buildings. The school closed down in early 1945. Before the school closed, cadets there had logged more than 200,000 flying hours with only two fatalities.

At Chapman Field in Miami, young women received primary flight training from the Embry-Riddle operation before being assigned to Avenger Field at Sweetwater, Texas. Four female instructors were employed by Embry-Riddle from 1942 to 1945. WASPS (Women's Air Force Service Pilots) were taught at the seaplane base in Miami. Officially known as the Embry-Riddle operation it was located at the Hotel Fritz in Miami. Many military pilots who fought in aerial combat during World War II owed their expertise to the civilian pilots who patiently took their cadets through primary training at many of the civilian schools in Florida.

Chapter Six

The Allied Airmen

After December 7, 1941, fighting a two-ocean war under the leadership of Franklin D. Roosevelt, the United States signed an agreement with fourteen of its allies called the Lend Lease Agreement. It provided for reciprocal aid and the pooling of human and material resources directed toward a common goal — winning the war. It was the aspect of "the pooling of human resources" that had already been placed into action.

When Germany began to put the lights out in Europe in 1940, much of the world shrank in horror and waited for the invasion of England. The British and remnants of the French armies had been miraculously evacuated from Dunkirk. Shortly thereafter, the Swastika flew over Paris and Hitler reviewed his victorious troops on the Champs Elysees. It did not bode well for England. It seemed as though England might have to stand alone against the onslaught of Hitler's armies.

In the skies over the channel ports and airfields, the Luftwaffa decimated the British fighter squadrons and bombers destroyed the airfields. Aircraft could be replaced relatively quickly, but pilots required time — time for training, time to develop gunnery skills, time to develop navigational skills and time to learn new combat air tactics, but time was running out. The solution lay in the United States. Late in 1940 top-ranking aviation experts from Britain, Canada and the United States met in New York to explore possible solutions. The question of how to go about training pilots for the Allies lay in the private civilian air schools. Would such a program of aid violate the already shaky neutrality of the United States? The decision was made to go ahead despite the problems of neutrality. American private flight training schools would train Allied airmen, as discussed in the previous chapter, producing pilots capable of flying a variety of fighter and bomber aircraft. Once training was complete, the pilots would be rushed to the defense of their homeland.

Arriving in small numbers at first, they came from Australia, England, Canada, India, China, South Africa, Norway, Czechoslovakia, Greece, France, Brazil and Poland. Many of the pilots from the British Empire wore the uniform of the RAF, which included many trainees from Poland and Greece. They were shipped to Embry-Riddle schools at Dorr and Carlstrom airfields, to Greenville Aviation at Ocala, Lodwick Aviation Academy at Lakeland, Riddle-McKay Aero College at Clewiston, and the Orlando Aero School. All these schools shared in training the eager young Allies.

In late December 1940, military personnel from Central and South America arrived to receive primary and intermediate training in Florida. They came from Brazil, Cuba, Ecuador, Bolivia, El Salvador, Paraquay, Uraquay, Nicaragua, Chile, Venezuela and Argentina. All went directly to the Embry-Riddle Air School at Miami.

Photo: Arcadia Historical Society
British cadets arriving at Carlstrom Field

When Germany made its fateful and disastrous decision to turn east and invade Russia, it was not long before U.S. military bases were seeing the coarse wool uniforms of Russian servicemen.

The British training schools were rushing their training timetables in order to put pilots in the cockpits of fighters. In the U.S. the flight training for the allied airmen usually consisted of ground school and aircraft familiarization, ending with a total of 200 hours of flying time. More flight time was added at intermediate flight schools, more at tactics schools, etc. Some pilots returned home to become instructors, whereas others were assigned to the Air Transport Command and ferried a variety of aircraft to wherever they were needed.

Cadets were put through the rigors of aerial combat training, cross-country navigational flights and night flying problems. Many young men training with the RAF died during the stress of pilot training. Twenty-three cadets who died during training at Arcadia are buried in the city of Arcadia's Oak Ridge Cemetery. Arcadians still hold commemorative ser-

A technical division was established to deal with the new students and the many languages they brought with them. This division was located at the so-called Fritz Building or Aviation Building which had been a large hotel until the war. This was months before citizens of Miami came to expect the variety of new uniforms in restaurants and in the many public places.

In addition to being in a country free from the daily bombing by German, Japanese or Italian aircraft, the Allied servicemen enjoyed the plentiful food and clean quarters. Generally they were eager and willing students.

Upon completion of basic flight school training, the pilots were sent to intermediate training facilities, some of which were located in Florida. NAS Pensacola, Jacksonville, Miami, Daytona Beach, Deland and Melbourne trained Royal Navy pilots, especially in carrier and over-water exercises. The Army airfields conducted fighter and bomber training at Fort Myers, Sarasota, MacDill, Avon Park, Lakeland, and accommodated radar guided aircraft at Boca Raton and maintenance instruction at Venice and Eglin. Altogether throughout the United States, the Allied pilots received training at 62 civilian schools and 150 military facilities. England no longer seemed to stand alone against Germany.

Photo: Arcadia Historical Society
British pilot trainees and instructors at Carlstrom Field

vices each Memorial Day.

One such British student pilot, training at the Lodwick school of Aeronautics located at Lakeland, became a German Prisoner of War. Taking off from Lakeland, the young cadet was busily flying about in a Stearman biplane when he received instructions to land because of an approaching thunderstorm from the west. He was directed to fly toward the foul weather in order to remain upwind of the airfield.

The pilot acknowledged his orders, flew toward the storm and promptly disappeared. The Civil Air Patrol was notified as well as the coast Guard. Search parties failed to locate any trace of the aircraft. A few weeks later a trawler working the fishing banks off Alabama, located the wreckage of an aircraft that contained the serial number of the missing Stearman. It was officially reported that the RAF student had crashed into the Gulf of Mexico and drowned. No trace of the pilot was found and further search was cancelled.

At the end of the war in Europe, interrogation of released RAF prisoners of war revealed a prisoner with a most unusual reason for being a POW. Verification of this story proved this was the young pilot who disappeared in the Stearman. Circling what he thought was the same position (without radio contact), he ran out of fuel and was forced to ditch in the Gulf of Mexico. He had no idea where he was or how far from land. He was able to extricate himself from the wreckage and floated in the Gulf. About an hour later with the sun in the afternoon sky, a German submarine that witnessed the crash appeared and plucked the pilot from the water. Taken aboard the submarine, he eventually went to Germany where he was interned at a Luftstag prisoner of war camp.

Photo: Arcadia Historical Society

RAF monument to fallen pilots

With a system of excellent technical schools, numerous basic training classes in camouflage, engine repair and assembly, aircraft identification and instructors classes located at Venice Air Base, what better facility to send Allies for training? On January 16, 1996, about 400 men of the 14th Chinese Service Group arrived at the Army station for training by the parent 4500 Service Group. They remained at Venice Air Base until October 2, 1944 at which time they returned to China.

The Chinese troops were a source of great interest and curiosity by the local citizens of Venice and surrounding communities, especially the first few weeks after their arrival.

Photo: Lakeland Historical Society

RAF crewmen in training with P-39 at Lakeland AAF

Always polite and rarely in trouble, and because of their distinct difference in nationality, the Chinese will be long remembered by all those who knew them.

Based at Chevalier field at NAS Pensacola, 59 French Navy pilots and 2,775 Royal Navy pilots received invaluable pilot training from primary to intermediate training. Eventually many of these pilots went on to receive fighter pilot training with F4F Wildcats, F5P Hellcats and the one aircraft the British especially liked, the F4U Corsair.

Allied pilots were also sent to many of the Army fighter training facilities. One such pilot was Waiter Czajkowski, a young Polish officer serving with the RAF. He wrote: *When Germany invaded my homeland, I was in Great Britain studying to be an instructor pilot, using RAF fighter planes. In the middle of March 1940, I was sent to Canada with 23 other pilots for training and from there they finally sent us to Eglin. They did not know what to do with us, so we were then sent to Marianna, Florida. After 3 weeks of advanced single-engine checkout they discovered we were really capable pilots. The basic problem we all seemed to have, we could read English well enough to get through the mountains of manuals we had to deal with, but when it came to speaking... that was a different story.*

From Marianna, we were then sent to Page Field at Fort Myers, Florida. There we were introduced to the P-39. I personally thought the P-39 to be a terrible airplane, but others thought differently. I really enjoyed the Fort Myers area as the town folks were very good to all the servicemen who were stationed there. We established a routine of daily flying, mostly navigational types, all over the Florida countryside. When we had time off, we RAF pilots were allowed to take up one of the many Stearman trainers. One beautiful day I was given permission to take up a Stearman and make a navigational flight to a place called Basswood Estates, outside the town of Okeechobee, to fly over the small grass airstrip, get new bearings and return to base. I did all that, except outside of a small place called Babcock, the radial engine decided to swallow a piston. When I looked behind me and saw that line of blue-white smoke and felt the shaking of the plane, I knew what had happened. Unfortunately the RPMs were dropping and I kept losing altitude.

I decided to put the aircraft down instead of pushing my luck. Below me for miles was nothing but grazing land and so I selected what looked like a reasonable piece of land to put down the Stearman. I think the engine seized just as the wheels bounced the first time. My landing was somewhat uneven as the ground was not very smooth, but I managed. I was standing beside the smoking aircraft when I saw a Ford platform truck coming across the grass. Two fellows stepped down and asked me if I was all right, and in my excited broken English, replied, 'Yes, I am.' They asked who I was and I told them I was Polish, flying with the RAF. It was too absurd for them and one of them came up with a shotgun from behind his back. He told me to get into the back of the truck and they drove me to Babcock where I was handed over to the local police. After locking me in his jail cell, he made telephone calls to Page Field, as I indicated, and satisfied I was real, he released me.

I was then taken to someone's house. The family there spoke some Polish, although they were German. We had a wonderful time. We ate and drank, and ate and drank, all good German food but so good. Later the next morning the Army MPs came and took me back. Yes, because of that I come here every winter now. Good place, Florida.

Greek RAF pilots training at Lakeland soon discovered the large Greek community at Tarpon Springs. Indian, Czech and French pilots remember Orlando and the Orlando Air School as well as the Rollins College at Winter Park. Some folks remember the young men with the RAF blue flying togs. Others were totally unaware of them. Many residents of St. Petersburg remember the Mexican Navy officers who were trained in anti-submarine warfare at the Naval Air Station (the Coast Guard Air Station of Whitted Field).

Chapter Seven

Women In Uniform

My name is Margaret Louise DeVaney. Army serial number 0407811. I was 31 when I joined the Army. I was working at the Opa Locka Naval Air Station in Opa Locka, Florida on Pearl Harbor day. What pandemonium rained that day. Shortly after that my husband went overseas with the Army Engineers as a civilian employee. At the time I was employed at the Naval Air Station driving busses and dump trucks. I was recruited in November and sworn in on December 7, 1943 at Miami Beach.

I was immediately sent to basic training at Fort Oglethorpe, Georgia. Upon completion of basic training, I was sent to Eglin Field, Florida. It was a very desolate area. We were the first group of women to wear the Army Air Force patch on our uniform.

Women worked in all departments — parachute rigging, radio repair, tower operators, dispatchers, cooks, dietitians, medics as well as shoe repair and clerk typists. I am proud to have served my country during World War II.

Photo: US Army

WACS in training at NAS Daytona Beach

Margaret DeVaney was one of over 200,000 women who served in the Army as a WAAC. Public Law 554, approved on May 14, 1942, created the Women's Auxiliary Corps as part of the regular Army. The purpose of the WAACs was to make available to the Army, for the duration of the war, the skills and special training of qualified women.

Mrs. Oveta Gulp Hobby, a former Texas legislator and civic leader was named WAACS Director on May 14, 1942. She held the rank of Colonel, the first United States woman to do so. Initially the armed services were less than enthusiastic about accepting women; however the idea of enrolling large numbers of women became compelling as the need for more and more personnel increased. Under the slogan, "Free a man to fight," more than 350,000 women would serve in uniform.

WAACs served at more than 400 Army and Army Air Corps installations, and were involved in 239 non-combat Army jobs. 18,000 served overseas in 21 different countries. In September 1943, the Women's Auxiliary Corps (WAACS) became the Women's Army Corps (WACS).

WAACS were first trained at Fort Des Moines, Iowa. As the number of women increased, a second training facility was opened at the newly-constructed NAS Daytona Beach. During the summer of 1942 Daytona Beach was a single industry town — tourists. Then, by carloads and trainloads, women military personnel began to arrive in Daytona Beach. Hotels and apartment houses were hurriedly altered to provide housing and mess areas for the WAACS. It was easy to spot WAAC structures by the wooden fire escapes and by the signs, "Military Reservation — Restricted."

Although the hotels housed large numbers of women and were utilized for special training, two miles west of the city, a tent city was constructed to care for some 7,000 WAACS. South of the city, on the west bank of the Halifax River, a small city of tents housed the Reception and Staging Battalion. Newly-arrived recruits were processed and indoctrinated for three days, then sent to Tent City.

Once they completed four weeks of basic training they would once again return to the Staging Battalion and await orders that would send them to service at a military base. The WAACS presented a sharp military appearance on the streets of Daytona Beach. One could even recognize a WAAC in cities. They were fine soldiers — neat, trim, precise and military in all respects.

The citizens of Daytona Beach were proud and protective of "their girls." The city did everything possible to add to the comfort of the women, making their short stay enjoyable. All resort facilities were turned over to the WAACS and the recreation room at City Island became a service club. Daytona Beach was as military as any Army training facility, but it was certainly easier on the eyes. There were thousands of WAACS there, with thousands of new recruits arriving every ten weeks.

Margaret DeVaney received her training at Ft. Oglethorpe, Georgia. Upon completion of training, she and a detachment of fellow trainees were sent to Eglin Air Force Base at Valparaiso. There she was assigned to a weather detachment and served in that capacity until she was separated from the service.

The lasting and popular image is the WAC serving as a driver for some handsome officer or as a clerk-typist. They did these and 237 other military jobs.

For Jan Goetz of Sarasota, serving as a WAC meant going off to war in far-off New Guinea on October 10, 1944. From there, with all the mud, rain and biting mosquitoes in December of 1944 she and a few others were ordered to Leyte in the Philippines. Leyte also proved to be a land of foxholes, mud, mosquitoes, and roaring typhoons. Goetz then vent on to Manila to serve with U.S. troops under the command of General McArthur.

Congress amended the Naval Reserve Act of 1938 on July 30, 1942, establishing the WAVES. On August 3, 1942 Mildred H. McAfee became the first woman to be sworn into the Navy under this Act. Prior to this she was president of Wellesley College in Massachusetts. Holding the rank of Lieutenant Commander, McAfee served as the director of the WAVES until February 1946.

The appointment of women officers generally involved the same standards as for male serving officers, however, it should be noted, the educational standards of enlisted women were much higher than those prescribed for enlisted men. Physical requirements were slightly different from the men.

The first Officers Candidate School (OCS) was established on the campus of Smith College in North Hampton, Massachusetts. Officer and enlisted schools were scattered throughout various college campuses, from the Massachusetts Institute of Technology to the University of Chicago to the University of California. WAVES were trained in Japanese, air navigation, aviation radio, gunnery, photo interpretation, Link Trainers, radio, yeomen, cooks, hospital corpsmen, machinists mates, aviation repair, engine repair, parachute riggers and many other jobs. Approximately 150,000 women served in the Navy during World War II.

Many fine young women were sent to Florida and served in a variety of capacities. In January 1943, the first contingent of WAVES reported to the Naval Air Station at Jacksonville. This initial group was composed of storekeepers, yeomen, communication personnel and many seapersons. In the early days of the war, WAVES were quickly assigned to desk work. As the need for more skilled personnel increased, Navy women were working in 38 different ratings. They served at NAS Jacksonville as radio persons, cooks, parachute riggers, photographers and aviation mechanics. They were excellent instructors in aerial navigation, Link trainering and gunnery.

Training at the Navy's specialized schools for WAVES duplicated that of men in order that the women would be prepared to perform the same duties. With this type of preparation, WAVES were soon being assigned duties at all Navy air stations, such as Pensacola, Melbourne, Fort Lauderdale, Vero Beach, Key West and Richmond.

The WAVES became completely integrated into the regular Navy and Naval Reserve in 1948, and today can be found serving on combat vessels.

The images of a young woman at the controls of

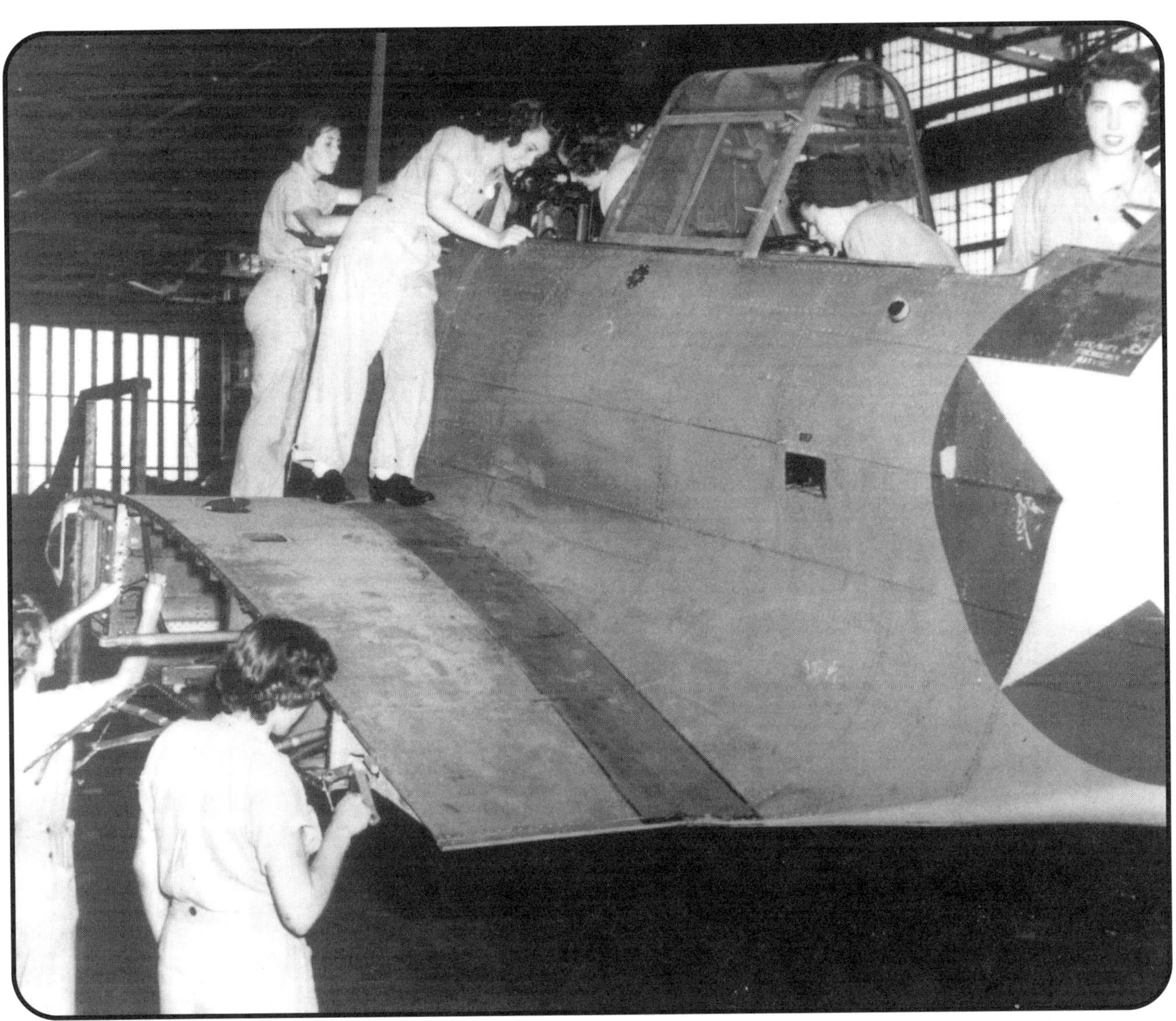

Photo: US Navy

WAVES aviation metalsmiths at work in the Assembly and Repair Department, NAS Jacksonville

Photo: Jean Cummings Collection
Female aircraft transport pilot

a Superfortress B-29, a Flying Fortress B-17 or a super fast Mustang P-51 or a P-47 Thunderbolt is one that, despite several good works of literature, remains little known by the public. For more than two years women served with the U.S. Army Air Forces (AAF) as pilots and their contributions to the war effort was immeasurable. They proved to the world that they were capable, and could be trained in large numbers as proficiently as male pilots. Gender bias in aviation was ill-conceived and based in large measure on ignorance.

Two very different groups of women pilots made their marks during the war — the WAFS (Women's Auxiliary Ferrying Squadron) and the WASPS (Women Air Service Pilots). The more experienced women pilots gravitated toward the WAFS directed by Nancy Harkness Love, an experienced woman aviator. WAFS were assigned to Ferry Command and spent most of their flying time ferrying every type of war plane to various air bases throughout the United States and eventually to selected overseas bases.

The WASPS, enlisted pilots that were less experienced, went through pilot training as did the men. Jacqueline Cochran, the famed woman pilot from Florida, was appointed Director. The first class of WASPS was trained at the Embry-Riddle School located at the so-called Seaplane Base in Miami. At the Seaplane Base women who wanted to join the WASPS were allowed to build up flying qualification time before being sent to Avenger Field at Sweetwater, Texas. From Texas, pilots were sent to different specialties

Photo: Jean Cummings Collection
Women pilots in training, Avenger Field, Sweetwater, Texas

Photo: Jean Cummings Collection

WASP pilot towing gunnery pratice target sleeve

within the Air Force. Some served as test pilots at Gardner Field in California. So pleased was the Commanding Officer with the women's attitude and competence, he had no reluctance having them fly the most hazardous assignments.

WASPS not only flew training planes and the big bombers, but also tow target planes. Many a WASPS pilot felt the shattering experience of bullets ripping through her aircraft as inexperienced gunners sighted on her instead of the target sleeve.

When morale among the infamous B-26 pilots (mostly men) hit an all-time low, something dramatic needed to be done. "One a day in Tampa Bay," was the saying uttered by the B-26 pilots stationed at MacDill Air Base near Tampa. In a single month, 15 B-26s crashed in the waters of Tampa Bay. In the fall of 1943, at a training base located in Alabama, the entire base complement was paraded on the flight line. What followed was considered by all spectators to be a spectacular air show staged by two B-26s. Afterward when the two medium bombers landed and taxied to the formation, four WASPS climbed from the cockpits. Grumbling among the male pilots quickly ceased. WASPS flew planes to and from every Army Air Force base in Florida.

Public Law 773, November 23, 1942, authorized the Women's Reserve of the U.S. Coast Guard Reserve. The SPARS (taken from the motto of the Coast Guard *Semper Paratus*, Latin for "Always Prepared") enlisted 13,000 women during the course of the war. Captain Dorothy C. Stratton, Dean of Women at Purdue University in Lafayette, Indiana, was appointed Director of the SPARS until 1946. The SPARS were integrated into the Coast Guard service in the shortest possible time, and this occurred with little difficulty.

Enlisted women personnel eventually were trained at the recruit training base at the U.S.C.G. station at Palm Beach. Upon completion of basic training, the SPARS remained at Palm Beach for specialist training as yeomen, cooks, store keepers and supply officer's school.

One of the recruit training facilities in Florida was located at St. Augustine. Young men and women were trained at the Hotel Ponce de Leon. There was an average of 2,000 to 3,000 men and SPARS stationed at this training facility. The Ocean View Hotel, located on the bay front, served as home to many SPARS. A large number of women were also attached to the Public Health Service located at St. Augustine.

The largest training school for recruit SPARS was located at Palm Beach. It was part of the greater Coast Guard recruit training camp and schools located in Palm Beach. Thousands of men and women were trained here, and upon completion of their training were sent to other schools located in Florida or other parts of the country.

The Marine Corps was the last service to enlist women. Unlike women in other branches of the Armed Forces, the women Marines had no catchy acronym, such as the WACS or WAVES, instead they were called like the men — "Marines." With women authorized to serve in the Marine Corps in 1943, approximately 23,000 women did so.

These Marines received regular basic Marine boot camp training and weapons training. Duties consisted of those carried out by women in other military branches. The need for more and more combat personnel, especially the island-hopping Marines, required replacements at various Marine bases. Women Marines fulfilled this role extremely well. The performance of women Marines was outstanding, despite the extreme initial harassment.

Shortly after the turn of the century the Army Nurse and Navy Nurse corps were formed. They were not considered actual organizations of the armed forces. This status quickly changed with the advent of World War I. The Army Nurse Corps quickly grew from 400 to approximately 20,000.

Many served with medical units stationed in England or France. It was during this period when women in the services were taken seriously, especially the "Angels in White."

60,000 women served as officer nurses during World War II. They were in Army hospital units in all theaters of war. Lest we forget those wonderful Army Nurses who served at Bataan and finally Corrigador, many from these units went on to die in the brutality of the Japanese concentration camps.

In Florida, Army Nurses were assigned to base hospital units, convalescent hospitals, dispensaries, health and sanitation units and many other necessary medical facilities.

Vivian Sheridan remembers, *...wading onto Omaha Beach, June 6, 1944, past the wreckage of burning boats and, I hate to say this, using bodies for a shield. Our small unit of nurses landed on Omaha Beach in the middle of the afternoon in broad daylight because of the number of severely injured soldiers. We had hard hats on, but there was a lot of exposed body under that hat. When we got the chance, we'd dash out and give a wound soldier a shot to ease the pain. That was about all we could do. There was no way we could set up a hospital.*

Ms. Sheridan is one of the many military nurses so fondly remembered by combat veterans.

Authorized by an Act of Congress on May 13, 1908, women were permitted to serve as Navy nurses in hospitals, and around 1920 began serving aboard hospital ships. Recruiting for qualified women nurses began in 1939 as part of the preparations for the war. At peak strength, about 14,000 women served as officer nurses. Many served at base hospitals and others at traditional Navy medical facilities within the continental United States. Many others served as medical personnel on hospital ships in all theaters of the war. During 1943 Navy nurses were trained in air evacuation which greatly enhanced the potential for survival of the severely wounded, especially the Marines fighting in the Pacific.

The performance of women in uniform during World War II was considered outstanding. They served in every theater of the war, and withstood considerable harassment and ridicule while serving capably.

Chapter Eight

The Submarine War

In 1939, just four months after Germany invaded Poland, the U.S. Congress was still protesting the involvement of the United States in any foreign entanglements. "We must maintain our neutrality," was one legislative expression. The war, however, was coming closer and closer with each passing day.

On December 19, 1939 a German freighter, the *Arauca*, steamed into Port Everglades as a means of escaping the British cruiser, the *Orion*. The *Orion*, fully involved with World War II, was attempting to capture the *Arauca* and its cargo as a military prize. The freighter remained in port until April 1, 1941 when it was seized by the United States as a belligerent, under an international agreement that limited the amount of time a belligerent could remain in a port and undergo repairs. The United States removed the crew and isolated them at the Coast Guard Base #6 at Fort Lauderdale Beach. After a week, the crew was shipped to Ellis Island in New York Harbor.

Throughout the early years of the war, German submarines wreaked havoc with Allied shipping, sinking thousands of tons each month, depriving England of much needed war materiel. With the Japanese bombing of Pearl Harbor, Hitler in turn declared war on the United States. In anticipation of war and to deal with the U-boat sinkings, the U.S. Navy established the North Atlantic Coastal Frontier, commanded by Rear Admiral Adolphus Andrews. Eventually this command would absorb the Southern 6th Naval District, extending the Coastal Frontier to northern Florida. Similar commands were established for the Gulf of Mexico, the Caribbean and the Panama Canal Zone. The new Eastern Frontier would be joined by the Army's Northeast Defense Command, the First Air Force, Coast Guard, Coastal Artillery and whatever else could be mustered to protect the vast eastern coastline. It would not be an easy task.

There were no fast, fleet destroyers (DD) or destroyer escorts (DE) to render effective anti-submarine warfare. The speedy destroyers had been removed and assigned to the Pacific in late December 1940. Small craft such as cutters and Navy patrol craft (PC) of 110 to 165 ft. were pressed into service. Small craft such as these, however, were no match for a German submarine sitting on the surface. On May 23, 1941, Admiral King ordered all Sea Frontier commanders to utilize small craft for coastal picket patrol. Often referred to as the "Hooligan Navy," this selection of privately-offered yachts of varying sizes and types would come to be officially known as the "Corsair Navy."

Originally the organization of this small boat force was given to the newly formed Coast Guard Reserve. The task proved too large for the reserve auxiliary, so the Coast Guard assumed responsibility. Yachts and power cruisers between 50 and 100 ft. were offered by their owners to the Navy, who in turn assigned them to the Coast Guard.

Almost anyone was accepted as a crew member, whether or not he/she could handle a small craft. After some time and training, the Coast Guard assigned regular crews to these boats. In Florida the Corsair Fleet was commonly known as the Mosquito Fleet — small boats with a deadly sting.

Patrol areas from Jacksonville to Key West to Pensacola were maintained along the so-called 50 fathom (300 ft.) curve off the Atlantic and Gulf coasts. Unless submarines were operating on the surface, they generally needed 50 fathoms of water in which to hide.

Each small craft patrolled about 15 nautical miles square. Most carried light machine guns, radios and depth charges. In addition to hunting submarines, the Florida Mosquito Fleet played a vital role in the rescue of survivors of sunken ships.

Photo: US Coast Guard

Coast Guard Corsair Fleet on patrol off Florida coast

Four months into the war, Admiral King authorized armed flights of civilian pilots in light planes of the Civil Air Patrol to become involved in anti-submarine patrols. All of these were to be stop-gap measures until the Navy could build enough of the 110-foot PCs. It was the small craft and light planes that would have to serve as the nation's defense against the terrible onslaught of the U-boats.

The Coast Guard was as concerned about shore lights as it was about small craft and called for an "Illumination Control Plan." This would include a blackout of all shore lights, beacons, lighthouses and all other aids to navigation, known to be exploited by the U-boat skippers. But for many communities, even in Florida, this plan was considered to be unreasonable. The majority of communities along the coast chose to ignore the plan because it would interfere with tourism and therefore business.

The Coast Guard pointed out that shore and port lights revealed passing shipping, providing an illuminated silhouette for searching U-boats lying in wait just offshore. At no time during the slaughter of shipping along the east coast of the United States was an entire blackout ordered. Many feel the civilian insistence for business as usual was as much responsible for the sinking of shipping as the German U-boats.

Early in 1942 with Naval and convoy defenses more effective in the North Atlantic, German U-boats moved south to waters off Florida and the northern Caribbean. Admiral Donitz of the German Navy, well aware of the lack of American coastal defenses and the disarray in the military's planning, took a calculated risk and initiated "Operation Drumbeat" (Paukenschalg). His plan called for the systematic sinking of Allied shipping that originated in South America. Oil rich Venezuela, Curacao and Aruba shipped tons of crude oil, gasoline and petroleum derivatives north through the western Caribbean, along the Florida east coast to ports in New Jersey and New York.

In the Caribbean Sea Frontier, Rear Admiral John H. Hoover had two old four-stackers (destroyers) a half dozen Coast Guard cutters of differing sizes and some patrol craft (PCs). Everyone suspected the submarines would do their dirty work in the Caribbean, but never off Florida's shoreline.

U-128 entered the waters of the Florida straits on February 1942 and promptly sank two oil tankers, one the British tanker *Eclipse* off Cape Canaveral. The next day another tanker was sighted off Bethel Shoals, the American tanker *Java Arrow,* and was promptly torpedoed and sank. Later in the same month, U-504 sank the oil tanker *Republic* three miles from Jupiter Inlet and a second, the Cities Services *Empire*, twelve miles northeast of the Inlet.

On April 9, 1942 during the early dark of night, U-123 quietly slipped past the town of Fernandia Beach into the mouth of the St. Johns River. Using the lights of the small towns and autos on the beach roads, the U-boat captain took his craft south past the mouth of the river, close to Jacksonville Beach. The wartime scene was eerie, everything brilliantly illuminated — a roller coaster, amusements, resort hotels and large numbers of autos with bright headlights. Proceeding south a few miles, the U-boat stopped and spent the night on the sandy bottom.

The next day, the U-boat now off the St. Augustine Lighthouse close to shore, its crew happily listened to American jazz music. Completely on the surface, U-123 moved north to Vilano Beach, just above St. Augustine. Here they spotted a huge oil tanker, the *SS Gulfamerica.* At approximately 10:00 p.m. U-123 fired two torpedoes, with only one striking the tanker. The sky erupted into a blinding flash of red and yellow flames. Not satisfied the crippled tanker would sink, the submarine decided to finish the job with its deck gun. It was point blank shooting and soon the tanker was sitting on the shallow bottom surrounded by a massive burning oil spill.

On shore the night's revelers watched in horror, unable to completely comprehend how a German U-boat could be so close to shore and sink a tanker without being detected beforehand. News of the sinking spread rapidly and soon the beaches were crowded by bewildered onlookers. Very quickly, Navy PBYs and Army B-25s from NAS Jacksonville were over the scene dropping magnesium flares, searching for the submarine. They never did find it. Florida's Governor Holland realized that the shore lights aided the sub in sinking the tanker, and ordered a blackout of all lights that showed seaward. This was never considered an adequate measure.

German Admiral Doenitz had promised Hitler his submarines would sink a total of 200 hundred cargo laden ships, one million tons, by April of 1942.

Photo: US Coast Guard

Tanker ablaze off coast south of Jacksonville

He sent more submarines into American waters. In slightly over one 24-hour period, his U-boats had sent six cargo ships to the bottom. Success would only be a matter of time. In these unprotected waters the Germans established a new record of slaughter.

Off the Florida coastline, German sailors lay about on deck of submaries and acquired suntans and enjoyed the warm air. Ashore the coastal communities were rife with rumors. People reported seeing German sailors dressed in uniforms sitting in movie houses, buying ice cream, or purchasing trinkets to take back home. There were reports of many small boats delivering fuel, milk and citrus fruit from a local dairy in St. Augustine, and food from beach front grocery stores. Reports of enemy spies and saboteurs poured into the local FBI offices.

On February 19, 1942 the tanker *Pan Massachusetts* was torpedoed and sunk about forty miles southeast of Cape Canaveral. Only 18 survivors were able to reach shore to safety. In that area, often described as the southern leg of the Bermuda Triangle between Florida and the Bahama Banks, 24 ships were sunk by German U-boats.

In May of 1942 the Mexican tanker *Portero del Llano* was torpedoed and sunk offshore of Miami. Shortly thereafter, the tanker *Faja de Osa* was sunk off the Florida Keys. Mexico, previously allied with Hitler, but a declared neutral, declared war on Germany. In late June U-boats had moved into the Gulf of Mexico. Torpedoes sank the British tanker *Empire Mica* off the coast of Apalachicola. In August German submarines sank the *Manzanillo* and the *Santiago de Cuba* running from Key West to Cuba.

Newspaper editors throughout Florida raged against the seeming freedom enjoyed offshore by German submarines. They demanded action other than small patrol craft and occasional anti-submarine aircraft. The Navy's answer was the slow-moving blimp. The lighter-than-aircraft was the most effective means of detecting submarines in shallow offshore waters. Blimp bases were located at Key West north to Richmond and NAS Banana River.

The United States Navy utilized some 200 lighter-than-air-craft in the war, mostly in anti-submarine duties. A blimp could remain over or near a convoy, searching for the telltale hulk of a submarine. Submarines under water generally traveled slower than surface cargo ships, so they would generally approach ships on the surface. Blimps proved to be relatively fast, about 80 mph. They could linger with a ship or convoy for long periods of time. They generally carried depth charges as well as iron bombs, however very few German submarines were sunk by blimps during the war.

Photo: US Navy

Coastal patrol blimp watching over US Navy tanker (AO-1080) off the Florida coast

Records show only one blimp, *K-74,* was ever shot down by enemy submarine fire. On July 18, 1942, while making a bomb run on the U-boat 134 south of Miami, the blimp was hit by small arms fire and slowly deflated. Seeing its chance to escape, the sub moved off leaving the deflating blimp to settle on the water. A nearby destroyer responded to the S.O.S. signal and rescued the ten-man crew.

With the establishment of training bases along the Florida coastline from NAS Jacksonville to NAS Key West and the increasing numbers of Navy PCs, by early 1943 the presence of the U-boats became too difficult for German Admiral Doenitz to maintain. Military aircraft in larger numbers now patrolled the waters off Florida on a routine basis. Florida's coastal cities, unlike most in the United States, experienced firsthand the savagery of unrestricted submarine warfare.

Chapter Nine

Spies Land In Florida

Throughout the country propagandists warned of listening enemy ears ("Loose lips sink ships.") and above all, "Beware of lurking spies." They were everywhere, not really, but it was made to seem so. When the Florida Defense Council in Tallahassee was activated, it directed local civil authorities to provide emergency firemen, extra police, medical teams, air raid wardens, air craft spotters and warning systems, blackout regulations, beach patrols and motorcycle escorts for the military convoys. The beach patrols would be on the lookout for submarines that might attempt to land spies and saboteurs. The motorcycle escorts would help escort police, medical teams and military convoys that would be passing through their communitics. Many an Army truck convoy was abruptly stopped by locals holding shotguns, who stepped from the darkness and demanded to know what their destination was. God help the officer who stumbled in his speech.

It was the local beach patrol who searched the dunes and the beaches day and night, looking for enemy activities on the sand until the military or the Coast Guard could take over the responsibility and produce the trained manpower. Eventually the Coast Guard beach patrols or mounted patrols would assumed the duty of securing the wide-open beaches of Florida.

In Berlin, Germany in 1942, Lt. Walter Kappe presented a plan to the Abwehr, the German High Command's intelligence group. Lt. Kappe offered a

Photo: Florida Archives

Typical Florida civilian motorcycle patrol, 1942

list of Germans who had spent many years living in the United States, and who spoke English without an accent. He suggested these men be trained to gather intelligence and act as saboteurs. For example, if they could dynamite factories producing war materials, Germany would reap tremendous psychological benefits. The plan was reluctantly approved.

The team received less than two months training at the sabotage school located in Brandenburg. Admiral Canaris, head of Security, reluctantly signed the orders releasing the men early for duty in the United States. The eight men were divided into two groups, the so-called Long Island Team and the Florida Team. Team One or the Long Island Team included George J. Dasch, Richard Quirin, Heinrich H. Heinck and Ernst Peter Burger. Team Two or the Florida Team was made up of Edward Kerling, Herbert Haupt, Hermann Newbauer and Werner Thiel. Thus began *Operation Pastorius.* It was a direct plan, one to damage industrial and transportation facilities of the northeast and middle Atlantic states.

A few minutes past midnight on June 13, 1942, U-202 surfaced off the coast of Amagansett, Long Island. Four men dressed in German Marine fatigues climbed into a rubber raft. They brought along four wooden crates and a sea bag. Within minutes they disappeared into the early morning mist. They were discovered by a Coast Guard patrol, and shortly after were arrested by the F.B.I.

On June 17, 1942, four days later, U-584 surfaced off the north coast of the Florida resort community of Ponte Vedra. Once again a rubber boat was lowered and the so-called Florida Team climbed in with all their gear and headed toward the surf crashing onto the beach. Unlike the Long Island Team, they were dressed in swim trunks (and military caps). Once on the beach, Edward Kerling directed the men to dig four holes in which to hide the wooden boxes. They completed the work and covered everything with beach sand. They had no way to communicate with the submarine nor the Fatherland since they had no short-wave radio. They were then to head north and rendezvous with Team One on Labor Day in Cincinnati, Ohio. Money certainly was no problem since Kerling carried more than $70,000 in his suitcase.

After burying the crates, they buried the shovels and their military caps. Picking up their three canvas bags, the four began the long walk toward Jacksonville Beach. Despite civilian beach patrols, they were not challenged.

The four saboteurs reached Jacksonville Beach around 11:00 a.m., still dressed only in their bathing suits. Locating the remnants of a stone wall, they quickly changed into dress suits and went in search of a bus that would take them to Jacksonville. Kerling and Haupt registered at the Mayflower Hotel under aliases. Theil and Newbauer followed suit and registered at the Seminole Hotel. After a hearty breakfast, they went on a sightseeing tour. Later they planned to take a train and make their way to New York to join up with Team One.

Alerted by George Dasch, the leader of Team One, the FBI responded swiftly. Kerling was already aware that he and the others had to move quickly and would have to be cunning to outwit the FBI, whom he knew would be searching for them and the others. Traveling now in two groups, he and Herman Newbauer checked into a New York hotel. The FBI

Photo: US Coast Guard

The Florida Four — German spies who landed near Jacksonville coast

had everyone known to Kerling in New York under serveillance. Kerling eventually was followed back to Newbauer where both were arrested.

Now only two of the eight spies were still at large — Herbert Haupt and Werner Thiel.

Even though the Abwehr had warned Haupt not to visit his former home, he returned to his old neighborhood to visit his girlfriend. The FBI was in no immediate hurry to arrest him, instead letting him roam about freely while he re-established his old contacts. Finally Washington sent word to arrest Haupt after he made contact with the remaining spy, Werner Thiel. The arrest took place at a roadside inn outside of Chicago. All eight saboteurs were now in custody, but one problem yet remained — the explosives of Team Two.

On June 24, 1942, seven days after landing, Keling and the FBI agents stood on the wide, sandy beach, 4.4 miles south of Ponte Verda Beach. Wearing handcuffs and leg irons, Kerling shuffled along the dunes that bordered Route A1A. Finally he stopped, pointed toward the remains of a house foundation and said, "There." The agents removed the covering sand and found the four wooden crates with explosives.

The FBI returned Kerling to Washington, DC to be incarcerated along with the other seven spies. The U.S. Government prepared its case thoroughly, and for a period of three weeks presented evidence to a select military tribunal which had been appointed by the President. In the end, all eight men were convicted and sentenced to death. Allowing six of the sentences to stand, President Roosevelt commuted the sentences of George Dasch and Ernest Peter Burger. Dasch was sentenced to 30 years at hard labor and Burger to life imprisonment at hard labor. In 1948 both men were deported to Germany.

Chapter Ten
The Coast Guard

During World War II, Arthur E. Smith served with the Coast Guard in Florida. He wrote:

When war broke out, December 7, 1941, I was a senior at Columbia University, in New York City, just 21 years of age. Immediately after the war broke out, I tried to get into the V-7 program of the Navy. It was a program that would allow individuals to complete college, and then go into an officer's training program. Unfortunately I could not get into the Navy at that time because I had high blood pressure problems and was therefore rejected.

I had a low draft number and did not feel that there would be an immediate possibility of being called up. I did want to join up, but wanted to join a service connected with the water, having always been around the water, from Long Island Sound. So I tried, after being rejected a number of times by the Navy, to get into the Coast Guard. I was accepted and was very pleased, mainly because I would have the chance to serve in small boats. Of course a small service such as the Coast Guard would offer a faster chance to rise in rank. I was able to complete my senior year of college and took technical courses for which I received graduate credits: a course in navigation and a course in electrical engineering.

I entered the Coast Guard Academy as a 90-day wonder, really, it was 120 days, on the first of October, 1942. In fact, as I entered my number came up with the draft. The first 30 days at the Coast Guard Academy was spent in Groton, Connecticut. The instruction primarily was based on the Monomoy, a type of unsinkable lifeboat, along with classroom instruction. The second 30 days was spent at the Coast Guard Academy at New London, where we worked with small craft and cabin cruisers which had been donated to the service. This provided me with the experience of handling small craft and learning how to "Conn" a ship in practice sessions.

The third month we went back to Groton where we operated with larger yachts, some 70-150 ft., which were also donated by the general public. This provided us with experience in operating larger vessels.

The fourth month we spent back at New London, where our class was divided into three groups: the upper third went to train on 83-foot small craft, the middle third went to the "Grand Mark," a Danish sailing vessel impounded by the U.S. when the war broke out. It was a three-mast sailing vessel. The bottom third went back to the small boats for more training. I was fortunate to get into the top third of my class and therefore trained in the 83-footers.

Upon graduation, I was assigned to the 1st Coast Guard District office with the Code Board, where we did coding and decoding work. Six months later, with the SPARS coming in, three of us volunteered to go to the 17th Naval District in Ketchikan, Alaska to establish a Code Board Communications

Office. This was around the time of the Japanese invasion of Attu, Kiska and the bombing of Dutch Harbor.

Duty in Ketchikan was boring, so I applied for and got a school located in Manhattan, New York. This was a ship's sanitation school and, as I lived in New York City, this was a great opportunity to be stationed near home. The school lasted for five weeks. Upon graduation I was assigned to the Tampa District at the Post Office building. The Coast Guard had small boats stationed at Davis Island and I lived in a hotel close by.

Every ship entering Tampa Bay had to be inspected for their boiler room and sanitary condition. We also inspected for proper lifeboats. This duty also included work at the TASCO shipyards. This duty only lasted for four months, when I was transferred to "USCG Calypso" as the executive officer. This 180-footer was out of Portsmouth, Virginia. They did anti-submarine patrols off of Cape Hatteras. This only lasted for a couple of months when I transferred to a Bouy Tender/Icebreaker, in the Chesapeake Bay area, as the executive officer.

In the last year of the war, I was transferred to Moorhead City, North Carolina, where I took command of the "USCG Ibisis," a 125-foot cutter just back from Greenland. It had a crew of forty and I was the only commissioned officer on board. We did air-sea rescue work, and anti-submarine patrols for Cape Hatteras. At the end of the war the ship was decommissioned and mothballed. I was discharged in May of 1946. I enjoyed the Coast Guard, the small number of men involved and the greater amount of responsibility. Since re-tiring my wife and I have moved to Venice, Florida.

With the arrival of the German saboteurs on Long Island and Florida, it suddenly became obvious just how vulnerable were the coastal areas of the United States. Most military officials realized that with the vast expanse of ocean, it would be difficult to invade the United States, but what about sabotage? Was it possible to land large numbers of saboteurs who could then roam the industrial heartland of the country and wreak havoc? The question of how to defend the vast open coastline troubled those involved with coming up with a solution. The solution would involve the Coast Guard.

The Coast Guard served as task force commanders landing craft flotilla commanders, convoy escort, combat beach masters and a variety of other capacities as needed. They also maintained their traditional duties of enforcing Customs, navigation rules and all Federal laws related to the high seas.

In early 1941, Coast Guard aviation planes became involved in anti-submarine patrols and convoy patrol. On November 1941, the Coast Guard was officially transferred from the Treasury Department to the Navy Department. By the close of 1942, the Coast Guard laid anti-submarine minefields, maintained a chain of rescue lifeboats, lookout stations, greatly increased beach patrols and in general kept the vast coastline of the United States under constant surveillance.

At the insistent urging of yacht clubs around the country, the Coast Guard accepted sailing and motorized yachts and quickly put them to use as

Photo: US Coast Guard

Coast Guard beach patrol along Florida Coast near St. Augustine

Photo: US Coast Guard

The Coast Guard Corsair Fleet of small boats

enlisted men as well as 360 officers and 10,375 men for fourteen Allied countries in 1942 and 1943. The so-called "Donald Duck Navy" replaced Florida's "Mosquito Fleet" and the Coast Guard's Corsair Fleet.

Coast Guard patrol units. It was a stopgap measure, but it worked. Dubbed the "Hooligan Navy," but officially known as the Corsair Fleet (as identified in Chapter 8), this array of small boats patrolled the coastline, often unarmed.

With large numbers of pleasure boats in Florida, owners there began the task of meeting the Navy's need for patrol craft. Yachts of 50 to 100 feet, with owners as captains and with pickup crews, were organized as part of the Navy's Eastern Sea Frontier defense. This "Mosquito Fleet," as they called themselves, patrolled the shallow coastal waters until the Navy could replace them with the standard 110-foot PCs. Dubbed the "Donald Duck Navy," because Walt Disney designed their logo, the PC Navy was trained at the Sub Chaser Training School at Miami. The school trained about 10,000 officers and 38,000

The threat of enemy submarines and their ability to place parties of saboteurs onto empty beaches still annoyed everyone. On July 25, 1942, Coast Guard Headquarters authorized all Coast Guard naval districts situated near a coastline to organize a well-armed and maintained beach patrol. Each patrol would operate as a part of the port security system.

The area to be covered by the patrol involved 3,700 miles of coastline. Foot patrols were supple-

Photo: US Coast Guard

Mounted Coast Guard beach patrol

mented by boat or motor patrols where needed. Normally foot patrols required men to travel in pairs, armed with rifles and flare guns. In secure beach areas, however, the armed patrols were only used at night. In areas of potential sabotage landings, around-the-clock surveillance was maintained.

The Coast Guard eventually, in August of 1942, added 2,000 dogs to the beach patrol and by September, horses were added to the mix. Many private citizens as well as Coast Guard personnel responded to the request for volunteer horsemen. One year after the order was issued there were about 3,200 horses assigned to the Coast Guard. Most of the mounted training took place at Elkins Park Training Station and at Hilton Head.

The mounted patrol did not patrol the more congested areas such as New England and New York. Instead, the mounted patrols were utilized to cover long stretches of more isolated beach areas. Very quickly the presence of uniformed young men made their appearance on the beaches, replacing the many civilian volunteers.

St. Augustine was one of the Florida cities to welcome the military. In 1942 one of the many Coast Guard training bases for enlisted men was located there as well as an officer's indoctrination school. Hotels, rooming houses and apartment houses were soon filled with young recruits. Florida's most famous hotel, Flagler's in Ponce de Leon, was utilized as the center for the Coast Guard Boot Camp. Housed on its exotic grounds was the mock ship, the *USCG Neversink.* It was used to train thousands of recruits in the basics of seamanship and navigation. There was so much to learn in such little time. The average stay for a recruit was from 6 to 12 weeks, dependent on the type of training involved. The training station contained 2,000 to 3,000 men and SPARS.

Small boats (50-80 footers) were used to familiarize the Boots with the feel and smell of the sea. A complete medical and dental facility had to be located at St. Augustine, staffed by doctors and nurses of the U.S. Public Health Service. The Hotel Bennet was used as a site for the Officer's Indoctrination School. The Hotel Monson became Headquarters for the Coast Guard Gunnery School. Various buildings and garages were taken over and became part of the school. The Hotel Marion became the headquarters for the Captain of the Port Authority. The municipal pier housed the local Coast Guard fleet of cutters and small boats.

Nearby Marine Studios and South Ponte Vedra also went to war serving the Coast Guard. Coastguardsmen also used the Castillo de San Marcos as part of the gunnery school, with some of its rooms used as classrooms. Several barracks were added to cover the overflow of personnel.

Photo: US Coast Guard

US Coast Guard Corsair Fleet, typical of the Florida "Mosquito Fleet"

In 1942 women were accepted into Coast Guard training and were sent to St. Augustine. The SPARS were quartered at the Ocean View Hotel, which coincidentally was next door to the Captain of the Port Authority at the Hotel Marion.

St. Mary's airfield served as an outlying field for NAS Jacksonville as well as a Coast Guard air station. A variety of Navy and Coast

Photo: US Coast Guard

Eight members of the coastal K-9 beach patrol

Guard aircraft were used to instruct pilots and crewmen in anti-submarine warfare and air-sea rescue techniques. In addition to the recruit training base, CG Beach Patrol Station #3, the 7th Naval District was located at Ponte Vedra Beach. There were dog kennels and stables there as well as at Marineland and Flagler Beach.

The beach patrol was highly concentrated from Jacksonville to Key West because of the number of military bases located close to the beaches. The men assigned to the Florida beach patrol were generally former residents of the state. This gave them a familiarity with the area not shared by others. In addition to vehicle, dog, horse and aircraft patrols, watchtowers were located on the outer beaches. The personnel at these towers were instructed to keep a lookout for light signals sent ashore by German submarines. The Coast Guard not only patrolled the beaches, searched for saboteurs, but they admirably rescued many survivors of sunken ships. The Coast Guard insured that America's shores were kept free from an enemy bent on destroying freedom.

Chapter Eleven

Civil Air Patrol

The idea for the Civil Air Patrol (CAP) was conceived as a means of enlisting volunteer civilian airmen for wartime duties. While the Navy rushed about supplementing its sparse anti-submarine forces, Admiral Andrews (Commander, Eastern Sea Frontier) gave thought to his woefully lacking air arm. Consisting of about 100 aircraft of varying designs and capabilities, three-quarters of these aircraft were not suited for the rigors of coastal patrol and anti-submarine warfare. The solution was to somehow involve the newly formed Civil Air Patrol until such time as suitable aircraft would become available.

Photo: Owen Gassaway

Typical CAP aircraft landing at Lantana Field, 1943

The Civil Air Patrol was organized a few weeks before Pearl Harbor and was comprised entirely of civilian pilots, many with their own aircraft. It was established as an organization of volunteer civilian pilots who would supplement military coastal patrols, especially in locating German submarines. The Army Air Corps, charged with the Coastal Air Defense, showed considerable interest and offered to utilize the CAP in limited over-water coastal patrols. On March 8, 1942, the CAP put a variety of private planes into the air — Cessnas, Wacos, Stinsons and Pipers were all utilized.

Meanwhile Admiral Andrews was still attempting to generate interest for a similar use of the CAP with the Navy. He reasoned that a "Scarecrow Patrol," if enough private aircraft could be used, would force the German subs to remain underwater. The Navy, in its cautious wisdom, rejected the idea on grounds it posed too many "operational difficulties."

It was left for the CAP to organize its official standing with the Army. The CAP thereafter remained under the command of the Army's First

Air Support, later with the Army's Anti-submarine Command's 25th Wing. Major General John Curry of the U.S. Army Air Force assumed command and with the most able assistance of Gill Wilson, the CAP flourished. In 1941 there were 128,360 certified civilian pilots, 14,047 light aircraft operating from 2,500 small to large airfields. Before the war would end, about 200 Floridians would participate in the all-volunteer air defense force.

One of these courageous civilian volunteers was Perry G. Snell, Jr., presently retired but Director of Volunteers at the Sarasota-Bradenton International Airport. He writes:

Born on the 2nd of April, 1926 and raised in Fort Myers, Florida, I was starting high school in the fall of 1942. Shortly after starting high school, I started taking flying lessons. I was sixteen and one-half years old. On October 18, 1942 I soloed and then joined the Civil Air Patrol. Due to the war, flying was restricted in Florida and as I wanted to fly, (which is why) I joined the CAP. This allowed me to get in some reasonable flying time. In October 1942, the order for the CAP Cadet Program was received and Fletcher Forehand, the Commander of the Fort Myers squadron, was directed to organize the program at the Fort Myers High School. To the best of my knowledge, with everything I have seen, I was the first CAP Cadet in the State of Florida. I believe there was only, at the time, one Master Sergeant rate for each state and I held that rank for the State of Florida, there being no commissioned rank in those days. I remember when the Army Air Force gave us the first military plane, an L-2, which we picked up at Lantana Field near West Palm Beach. I was able to fly from Lantana to Fort Myers in the back seat.

At Lantana I was able to see the CAP planes with their bomb racks attached. These planes were used for anti-submarine warfare as well as coastal patrol.

I had my first search mission with the CAP on July 18, 1944 when a Bell P-39 failed to return from a training mission out of Naples. We were unsuccessful on the first day of the search, but on the second day, while I was piloting the aircraft, Captain Kohler spotted the missing P-39 down amongst some thick trees. We attracted the attention of an Army BT-13 nearby and led them to the crash site. They, because of their low wings, did not see it but radioed Naples that they were certain we had. So we returned to Naples, located the site of the crash, loaded up with smoke bombs and headed to the wreck site, which was south of the Tamiami trail, and we led the rescue teams to the site. We had to go back the next day because the rescuers did not find the pilot in the wreck. Although we were unable to locate the pilot, he was found the next day not far from the wreck. He had bailed out too low for his parachute to open.

Our next mission was for a BT-13 missing from Punta Gorda. We made several searches and never did find it. To the best of my knowledge it was never found, like so many. Because we were flying on active duty, the pilot got seven dollars a day and the observer received five dollars a day.

The CAP also participated in a mock bombing raid on Tampa as a means of testing Tampa's civil defenses. Some of our pilots loaded paper bags with flour, flew to Tampa and dropped their flour bombs. The only report that one of the pilots had was that he was not sure of what he hit except one outhouse.

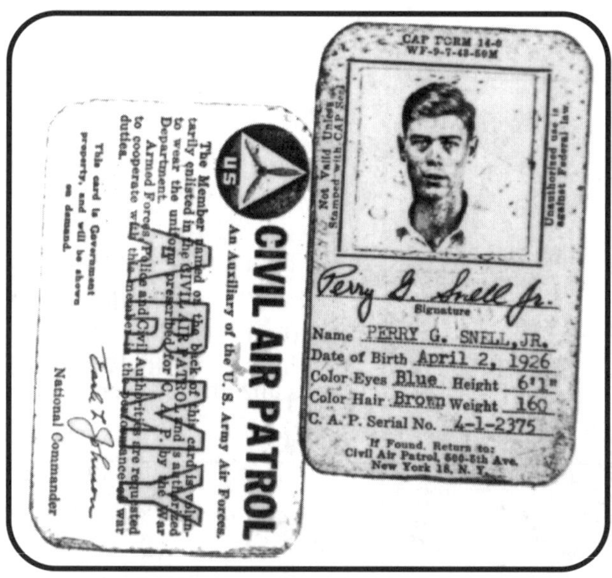

Photo: Perry G. Snell Jr.

Official CAP pilot registration card

These civilian pilots flew an estimated 12,000,000 miles on anti-submarine patrol, operating from 21 bases from New England to Texas. Units of the CAP recorded spotting 173 German submarines, attacked 57 and are credited with sinking two. Approximately 800 men and women flew more than 200 hours of combat patrol.

From March of 1942 until May 18, 1942 the

Photo: Owen Gassaway

CAP flight crews at colors, Lantana Field, 1943

CAP in Florida maintained a continuous two-plane air patrol over coastal beaches and shipping lanes within 60 miles of the coast. Some of the aircraft carried a single 325-lb. depth charge or two wing-attached 100-pound demolition bombs. These pilots flew in every kind of weather even sometimes when military pilots were grounded.

Photo: Owen Gassaway

Civil Air Patrol ensignia as utilized on light aircraft

Coastal residents and commercial fishermen became accustomed to seeing the low flying civilian aircraft with the CAP red or white triangular insignia. The presence of these brightly colored aircraft soon became the nemesis of the U-boat crews. The Germans referred to them as the "gelb die Biene," the "yellow bees." The U-boat commanders were unaware at first that these CAP patrol planes carried no weapons, and so would dive when caught on the surface. Soon they realized they were safe from these small aircraft and would leisurely submerge to escape the search by military planes. This would cost some U-boat commanders because some of these pesky yellow bees soon carried stingers — bombs or a depth charge.

Because the fear of a CAP plane being shot

down and its crew captured, a special uniform was provided signifying civilian status. These pilots and crews flew and maintained their own aircraft. The Army only supplied them with the necessary high octane aviation fuel.

In Florida the CAP operated in one of the most active areas for German submarines. These small planes kept an eye on coastal shipping from the Gulf Coast through the Florida Straits, north to Jacksonville. They operated from bases at Lantana (West Palm Beach), Miami, Flagler Beach, Daytona Beach, Sarasota, Fort Myers, Clearwater and Panama City. In addition to flying anti-submarine patrols, the CAP pilots flew courier missions, tow-target flights for anti-aircraft machine gun trainees, radar tracking at Boca Raton, and searchlight tracking drills. One fine example of their efforts, which later became their hallmark, was the search for downed aircraft, either over water or the wilds of Florida. From 1942 to 1944, the Florida CAP unit flew 18,000 hours in search and rescue, mostly for downed aircraft and pilots. There was a cost of these many CAP missions. Ninety aircraft were lost, with twenty-six CAP members losing their lives, and others injured.

Florida CAP Record:

Missions flown	86,686
Hours	244,600
Reports on submarines	173
Bombs dropped on subs	82
Special Sea Investigations	1,046
Vessels in distress	91
Enemy subs sank	2
Special Convoy missions	5,685
Aircraft search missions	2,865
Florida CAP Aircraft lost	90
Fatalities	26

Photo: Owen Gassaway

RIGHT: German submarine caught on the surface by a CAP aircraft off the Florida coast

BELOW: An overall view of Lantana Field used by the Florida CAP

Photo: Owen Gassaway

As more and more military aircraft became available, the Navy took over many of the CAP's duty, especially the anti-submarine patrol. During the war, direction of the Florida Wing came from the able leadership of Colonel Vermilya. There possibly has never been such a noble and yet audacious service as found in the Florida CAP during World War II.

Chapter Twelve

Wartime Industry

Jacksonville, Panama City and Tampa, like so many other cities, had suffered through the decade of the Great Depression. All three are port cities and, although once active industrially, each became stagnant during the 1930s.

The shipbuilding capacity of Tampa was important to the Navy. Tampa Shipbuilding and Engineering Company with its skilled work force, sought money from the Public Works Administration to fund the construction of a large 10,000-ton dry dock.

The Federal Government, aware that war clouds would soon place a demand for naval and cargo shipbuilding, encouraged shipyards to become involved in the anticipated increase in shipbuilding. The Merchant Marine Act of 1936 provided not only the impetus but the finances. Not only did the Tampa Shipbuilding and Engineering Company (TASCO as the company was called) complete the dry dock, but it was awarded an $8 million contract for the construction of four new cargo ships. Two thousand new jobs were created and the future

Photo: The Florida State Archives

Shipbuilding at the TASCO Ship Yards, Tampa, 1944

looked much brighter for Tampa than it had for the past ten years or so.

Of the shipbuilding yards located in Tampa, TASCO was the most productive, building a variety of naval vessels, ranging from ammunition cargo ships, destroyer tenders, coastal mine sweepers, destroyer escorts, cargo ships, repair ships and even many of the smaller coastal patrol craft (PCs). TASCO constructed a total of 494 "bottoms" and also was involved in the conversions of existing ships.

When the Japanese bombed Pearl Harbor, TASCO geared up to meet the demands of a wartime navy. For the next four years, workers of all ages and skills were sought out to provide the manpower necessary to produce ships. The demand for workers was so great, older skilled workers were now asked to return and work at wages better than their Social Security (per Social Security Act of 1935) benefits. Retired metal workers, tool and die workers, pipe fitters and welders were highly sought after.

As contrasted to the Depression when communities were encouraged to keep teenagers out of the job market in order to give the available jobs to family "breadwinners," now they were asked to contribute by taking part-time jobs. With the demand for more and more men in the military, workers for defense industries became scarce. The solution — women! With a need for 20,000 to 30,000 workers to meet the increased demand of the Gulf Coast shipyards, bringing women into the workplace seemed to be the answer.

"Wanda the Welder" or "Rosie the Riveter" were roles women were quick to assume, and soon thousands were working alongside men in heavy industrial jobs.

With the influx of thousands of workers, Tampa and other Florida cities' civic leaders were pressed to locate suitable housing. Added to the situation in many cases was the demand for more housing by nearby military installations. Many ideas were suggested including turning vacant factory buildings into suitable apartments and establishing trailer parks. Eventually the shipbuilding companies and the cities supplied municipal housing which helped alleviate some of the problem, but it was always crowded. In addition to the TASCO yards, Tampa Marine, located along the Ybor Channel, produced ninety-eight sea-going fleet tugs for the Navy. Bushnell-Lyons produced large, steel cargo barges for the Navy. The Navy, realizing the need to house personnel or troops in various war zones, converted many of the barges or lighters, into floating barracks ships.

The strangest shipbuilding yard located in Tampa was the Hooker's Point Yard. Matthew H. McCloskey sought to take advantage of the shortage of rolled steel used in shipbuilding by building ships made of concrete. McCloskey was the owner of a large construction company in Philadelphia. He reasoned that because of material shortages and the increased loss of shipping due to the German U-boats, the so-called "concrete ships" could substitute until enough steel became available. The concrete ship was not new, having been built in Florida during World War I.

Hooker's Point seemed ideal to McCloskey since it was located next to the Tampa ship channel and not far from the Florida Portland Cement Company. Plus the climate allowed for the proper curing of cement.

Construction began immediately, building everything necessary to produce concrete ships — administration buildings, warehouses, manufacturing shops of every description and, most of all, the large basins to hold the ships as they were built. The basins were 7,200 feet long, 82 feet wide and 27 feet deep, and lined with concrete. All the basins were connected to the ship channel by huge lock doors. Three 360-foot ships could be built at the same time. Once again there was a desperate search for workers, especially those who could work with cement.

The building of cargo ships with concrete got its start during World War I. Unfortunately they proved to be unreliable and often were too fragile for use at sea. McCloskey brought to the shipbuilding process new techniques used in building highrise buildings. For example, when sand proved to be too heavy in mixing with cement, engineers produced a light weight concrete using "Fuller's Earth." Fuller's Earth is a lightweight clay that has been used for many years in filters and as an absorbent for grease.

These "floating skyscrapers," as they were nicknamed, were powered by 3,500-hp engines and performed very well despite the rough handling they received. Several were sent to the Normandy invasion, where two were sunk off the beachhead to create a barrier seawall. Production of these concrete ships, however, came to a halt when Henry J. Kaiser could produce a "Victory Ship," the famed Liberty Ship, in about ten days.

The Gibbs Shipyards, located on the south side of the St. Johns River in Jacksonville, was the premier shipbuilder in that area. During the First World War, Gibbs built small naval ships. It was in the middle of an expansion of the yard when the war ended. All through the 1920s to 1940, the yard laid stagnate among unfinished construction. When contracts for small wooden-hulled craft increased, the yards and buildings were renovated to meet the challenge of World War II. The Gibbs yard was involved in the production of over a hundred different types of vessels from the PT boats to landing craft of every size and shape. The speedy wooden-hulled PT boats became the yard's specialty. Many of the boats were sent to the British as part of the Lend Lease program to aid in the on-going Channel war. These boats were used in all theaters of war for a variety of purposes. A PT training base was maintained at Mayport throughout the war. The use of millions of sea mines by both sides in the war required the use of many wooden-hulled mine sweepers — the so-called YMS, the Yard Mine Sweeper.

Prigg Boat Works at Miami also built a similar variety of small boats and ships. The best known was the 110-foot PC, the famed sub-chaser.

Ships constructed at the Wainwright Shipyard in Panama City also served in all theaters of the war. They built two particularly useful ships for the war effort: the famed Liberty Ship and the "T" tankers. The Liberty Ship, a cargo transport, was 444 ft. in length with three flush decks and 11,000 deadweight tons. The Wainwright Yard built 102 Liberty Ships. The Liberty Ship was capable of making 10 knots, fully loaded. The first Liberty Ship built at Wainwright was named the *E. Kirby Smith*. Six 6T-1 tankers, 500 ft. in length and 16,000 deadweight tons, were built at Wainwright.

In the early years of World War II, shipbuilding was the principal industry in Florida. With the increased need for foodstuffs, the citrus industry received a tremendous shot in the arm. From 1942-1945, the Federal Government requisitioned processed fruit for the military. Embattled England, unable to feed itself due to war destruction and the redeployment of assets, relied on vegetables and fruit from Florida.

Florida's range-fed beef output increased and its processed meats were shipped all over the world. Many G.I.s adjusted just fine to the Sunshine State's beef. Innovations in food processing resulted in the development of the frozen citrus juice concentrate process. Land was cleared and more vegetable crops were planted, processed and canned.

This rapid increase in agriculture production solved many problems for the military, but the

Photo: The Florida State Archives

Ship building at the Panama City Shipyard, 1943

need for more soldiers and sailors, and the drain on local manpower for the growing shipbuilding industry, proved near fatal for Florida's agriculture industry. Migrant farm workers deserted stoop labor for steadier better-paying employment at the shipyards.

To solve the labor shortages, the Federal Government Extension Service directed an emergency program which started in 1943 and ended in 1947. It encouraged young people, women and families to work harvesting valuable crops. At critical harvest times the program also beseeched military bases to provide needed labor. In one instance seven hundred men from Buckingham Field, Fort Myers volunteered their leave time to save the nearby potato crop. This scene was repeated often throughout agricultural Florida.

Many of the prisoners of war at Camp Blanding were sent to local military bases to relieve servicemen of duties. During critical harvest times, many POW volunteers labored in the fields and groves to save perishable food stuffs. POWs did everything from harvest peanuts, corn, tomatoes, beans, and cutting sugarcane to picking the citrus crops.

Part of the solution to the agricultural labor shortage came from foreign workers from places such as Mexico, Haiti, Jamaica and Central America. To house these foreign contract workers, Farm Labor Supply Centers were constructed throughout Florida. Benefits to these workers included highly prized medical care, housing, food and transportation. Most of the farm labor camps consisted of the typical, and now familiar, nine-man pyramidal tents. These tent cities were easy to construct for temporary accommodations. Agriculture discovered an inexpensive and plentiful supply of willing migrant workers and continued to import contract labor long after the war.

Photo: Lakeland Historical Society

Amphibious tractors being readied for shipment to the US Marine Corps, 1944

Photo: USDA

Agricultural tent city for migrant workers at Pahokee, 1944

While some companies were manufacturing food processing machinery, some food machinery companies were making war material. In Lakeland, the Food Machinery Corporation manufactured "Water Buffaloes." These amphibious assault personnel carriers were ordered in large numbers by the Navy for the Marines. These tracked vehicles (LVTs) were utilized by the Marines as they fought their way across the vast reaches of the Pacific island-hopping campaign.

More than 2,000 employees, working three shifts a day, produced thousands of the assault vehicles. At the end of the war, FMC returned to manufacturing citrus processing machinery.

Dooley's Basin and Dry Dock on the New River at Fort Lauderdale produced large mine sweepers, the valuable submarine chasers (PCs) and the ever-present high speed air-sea rescue boats. It was always a treat to watch the newly manufactured boats maneuvering through the heavily-silted New River channel. Many hours of watching were directed at crews trying to free stuck boats.

Many local manufacturers obtained government contracts and produced large numbers of radios and electronic equipment, tents and millions of ammunition shells. The H.A.K. Corporation produced more than 1.6 million 37mm and 50mm shells. The Goodwin Awning Company in Fort Lauderdale endeared itself to the foot-sloughing G.I. by providing over 250,000 pup tents and shelter halves as well as many other types of tents.

For the residents of Jacksonville, Tampa and others industrials cities, the end of the war did not mean a return to dependence on the tourist trade. Florida demonstrated it had a highly motivated workforce. Florida's industrial base continued to expand after the war (and to the present).

Photo: David Kerns

Women making rubber life rafts in Florida

Chapter Thirteen

Florida's POWs

Shortly after Japan bombed Pearl Harbor and Germany declared war on the United States, a number of German civilians living in some Central American countries were, by agreement, deported to the United States. Seen as a threat to the Panama Canal Zone, these Germans were isolated for the duration of the war. Until someplace more permanent could be located, the military intelligence community agreed upon Camp Blanding as a temporary interment.

Under close surveillance by special military police detachments, the men, women and children were confined in a stockade of the usual fencing topped with barbed wire. Housing consisted of pyramid tents each suitable for four persons. These prisoners came from Panama, Costa Rica and Guatemala. Imprisoned without trial, forced to wear ill-fitting Army fatigues, they certainly must have wondered what the future held for them.

With the onslaught of these civilian aliens, military athorities decided to continue utilizing Camp Blanding as a prisoner of war interment camp. These civilian prisoners were moved in the summer of 1942 to a new site that had been constructed about a mile from the original prisoner compound. Blanding had been selected as the main POW facility and processing center for Florida. Its isolated, rural location in northcentral Florida, approximately 40 miles southwest of nearby Jacksonville, made it an ideal location to house prisoners of war.

With the daring exploits of the German U-boats off the Florida coast, it was inevitable that some would be sunk. Rescued crews became prisoners and were sent to the Blanding POW compound. These were the first of many German prisoners of war to pass through Camp Blanding. Eventually German army prisoners would be housed along with the sailors.

The submarine crews were considered to be some of Hitler's most elite and highly trained in naval warfare, something that very much interested Naval Intelligence. They represented a captive and ready source of valuable technical military intelligence, and the prisoners in many direct and indirect ways were constantly interviewed for bits and scraps of useful intelligence. Blanding became one of the four Army facilities in the United States to house POWs. Maintaining four different camps allowed the intelligence departments to shuffle stubborn and difficult German naval personnel from camp to camp. This movement allowed the camp commanders to control problematic officers who sought to better control their men despite the camp administration and their confinement.

The first German army prisoners arrived at Blanding on November 5, 1943. The constant demand for labor played a role in increasing the numbers of prisoners in Florida.

The main compound constructed for the German prisoners was located one-half mile from the naval site. Later a separate compound was constructed for the Italian POWs. Most Italian POWs did not remain at Blanding, instead they were sent to satellite facilities. Housing consisted of hutments and mess halls similar to those used in the CCC camps in the 1930s. Contingents of 250-300 men each arrived at Blanding, bringing the POW population to 1,000 men.

Hardened veterans from Rommel's legendary Africa Corps had been sent to camps located in the interior of the United States. It was reasoned that this action would deter any possibility of escape. However, with the increasing numbers of prisoners, the Federal Government felt it was a good policy to keep prisoners dispersed throughout the various states, including Florida, and different branches of the armed forces.

The arrogance of Rommel's veterans led to violence that was typical of the early administration of POW camps. With little to do, these prisoners had too much idle time and trouble was to follow. Testing Camp Blanding's commander was a favorite routine of the prisoners. With a newly announced policy of "no work, no eat," prisoner ring leaders staged a strike on November 15, 1943. Transferring the strike leaders and other dissidents to Camp Alva, Oklahoma resolved the problem, but raised the question of what to do with such large numbers of prisoners in Florida. The Geneva Convention of 1929 prohibited the use of prisoners in any war-related or dangerous situations. This restriction was carefully observed to prevent any retaliation by the German military against Allied POWs. The only work the prisoners were involved in was maintaining their own facilities within the compounds.

Late in 1943, Senator Claude Pepper submitted a request for prisoner of war labor to aid in the state's agricultural harvest. Paul V. McNutt, Chairman of the War Manpower Commission, authorized seven auxiliary POW camps in Florida.

The rules of the Geneva Convention were strictly enforced. Only lower ranking enlisted men and other volunteers were allowed to work, and then only when they were supervised by their own non-commissioned officers. Prisoners who were incarcerated at other camps in nearby states were shipped to Florida to set up smaller satellite camps under Camp Blanding's command. Prisoners from Alabama were sent to establish a camp at Clewiston, Florida early in 1944 to aid in the harvest of sugar cane. It must be understood these POWs did not work for nothing. In return for their labor they received 80 cents per day. Remember, that this was 1944, — and the private employers paid a matching wage. Coupons or chits were also issued to each working prisoner which entitled him to purchase cigarettes, food and other personal items at the POWs camp exchange. The so-called satellite or branch camps were established at Dade City and Winter Haven where POWs labored in the citrus groves. When these 200-man contingents were transferred to the private sectors, not only did secure housing have to be provided, but also a complete detail of security guards.

Researching this book for material often took the authors into unexpected situations. The following is a condensed interview with a former German POW held at Camp Blanding. Not wanting his Florida friends to know he was a POW and honoring his request to remain anonymous, no identification is offered.

There was not a thing to do at the Army compound at Camp Blanding, other than the daily cleanup details or remain in one's bunk and read, and that gets tiring. I did not volunteer to do farm work. You see, I had lived in the city and the only real work I had ever done was in the Army. Being sent to a farm labor camp meant being out of the foolishness of Blanding. We were sent to Winter Haven and were housed in two concrete buildings, which I believe had been used for some type of fair. The entire area was fenced. They thought we would try and escape, he laughed, pleased with himself.

From there we went out daily, in Army trucks guarded by military police, to vast fields of beans, onions and those delicious red tomatoes. Everyday I ate many tomatoes until it became too uncomfort able to eat more. I spent much time in the latrine... yea.

Sometime in early January, just after Christmas, we started traveling to the big fruit orchard... ah. groves. I shall always see in my mind that day and seeing all those ripe oranges! I had not seen an orange since I was a lad before the war. The trees with all their fruit seemed to go on for many kilometers. It seemed impossible that a country at war could afford to grow so many wonderful oranges. I can remember thinking at the time, that it would be impossible for Germany to defeat America.

It could afford to grow oranges.

I picked and ate my way through each tree and during rest periods, people from the farms provided cold water or fruit juice. I could not get enough. It was like living in paradise, and they paid us to do all this. And here all the time the authorities worried that we would escape! Why?

With the dispersal of large numbers of POWs throughout Florida, fear of German escapees roaming the vast countryside increased. Apprehension of escapees was left to the Federal Bureau of Investigation. With the fear of the Gestapo ingrained in the POWs, it was hoped this would serve as a deterrent. Escapes were nevertheless attempted, but records indicate that all who tried were apprehended. Some were used as examples of what happens when one does escape, as the following story illustrates.

With the dark of night, two former Wermacht members escaped from the Camp Blanding compound. They wandered about the tangle of vines, brambles and dense brush for two days without food or water before deciding to give themselves up. Badly cut by the thick undergrowth, lacking drinking water, and hopelessly lost, they stumbled onto a dirt road. Finally, being discovered by a local civilian, they asked to surrender. Once back at Blanding, they were placed on display, paraded before the others to see what happens when you try to escape from Blanding. Word of mouth and the horrors they experienced spread the word that escape from that compound was futile.

This is not to say there were no further escapes. One daring POW managed to escape from Blanding hiding in a railroad refrigerator car. He nearly froze to death in the attempt. He was apprehended in Jacksonville, happy to still be alive. There were attempts from Kendall, Orlando, Clewiston, Winter Haven and Miami. Information regarding POW attempted escapes in Florida is scarce, and in many instances still classified by the military.

With the demand for more and more air crews and especially infantrymen in Europe, training camps were re-training many of their personnel and sending them overseas, creating a shortage of personnel. MacDill, Drew Field, Orlando, Miami, Homestead and Venice all required POWs to work in the mess halls and laundries. The Navy requested their share of prisoners. NAS Melbourne constructed a POW compound and housed 300 prisoners. They worked in the mess halls or laundry and did general grounds work. At Whiting Field, POWs were used to control soil erosion problems and worked at other construction projects.

The largest number of prisoners quartered outside Blanding was at NAS Jacksonville. In June 1945, as the war was winding down, 500 German POWs were transferred to Jacksonville. They were housed in a secure compound built at the Recruit Training Facility. By October of 1945 there were 1,645 POWs at NAS Jacksonville. Although many of the Navy air departments requested POWs, most worked at the base dump reclaiming valuable metal

Photo: US Navy

Recent arrival German POWs lined up for roll call at NAS Jacksonville

materials. Many feel the POWs' greatest effort was the building of the additional back nine holes of a golf course there.

By the conclusion of the war in Europe, twenty POW camps were located throughout Florida. Included were Camp Blanding with 15 satellite camps, Telogia with its enormous logging camp and Camp Gordon Johnston in Carrabelle. Nearby the abandoned lumber camp of Harbeson City, a POW camp was constructed to house 250 German POWs. Later as activity at Camp Johnston diminished, the POWs were moved to new quarters, one no longer involved with the amphibious program. All these prisoners were involved with the harvesting of logs for the pulp or lumber industry. A few escapes were attempted, but because of the wilderness, they generally wandered into one of the camp areas asking for food and water.

At the end of April 1946, 243 German POWs still remained at Blanding. By May all had been repatriated or transferred to a different facility. Florida's wartime experience with its 4,000 plus German POWs came to an end, but not completely. Many former prisoners grew to like what they saw of the Sunshine State and later returned to vacation in its sunny coastal resorts. Many returned to live here as citizens of the United States.

Chapter Fourteen
The Hurricanes

With so many air bases, training facilities, naval and army bases with thousands of personnel, the fear of hurricanes was ever present. It would be almost impossible to protect aircraft sitting on the ground during a major hurricane. Aircraft reconnaissance was established during 1943 as part of an early warning system. With the traditional methods of reporting — ships with radios at sea, reports from the Caribbean islands and commercial aircraft — the direction and intensity of tropical storms were often a hit or miss proposition.

On July 19, 1944 the first tropical storm of the season was spotted east of the Bahama Islands. It moved north and finally into the Atlantic. The hurricane of October 13, 1944 was first reported by the motorship *Silver Arrow* in the western Caribbean as a tropical storm. The hurricane moved north, crossed western Cuba and then headed for the low-lying island of Dry Tortugas. The eye of the hurricane was reported over Dry Tortugas from 3 to 5 p.m. on the 18th.

This hurricane alert was passed to all base commanders, and hurricane preparations got underway. All aircraft were immediately flown

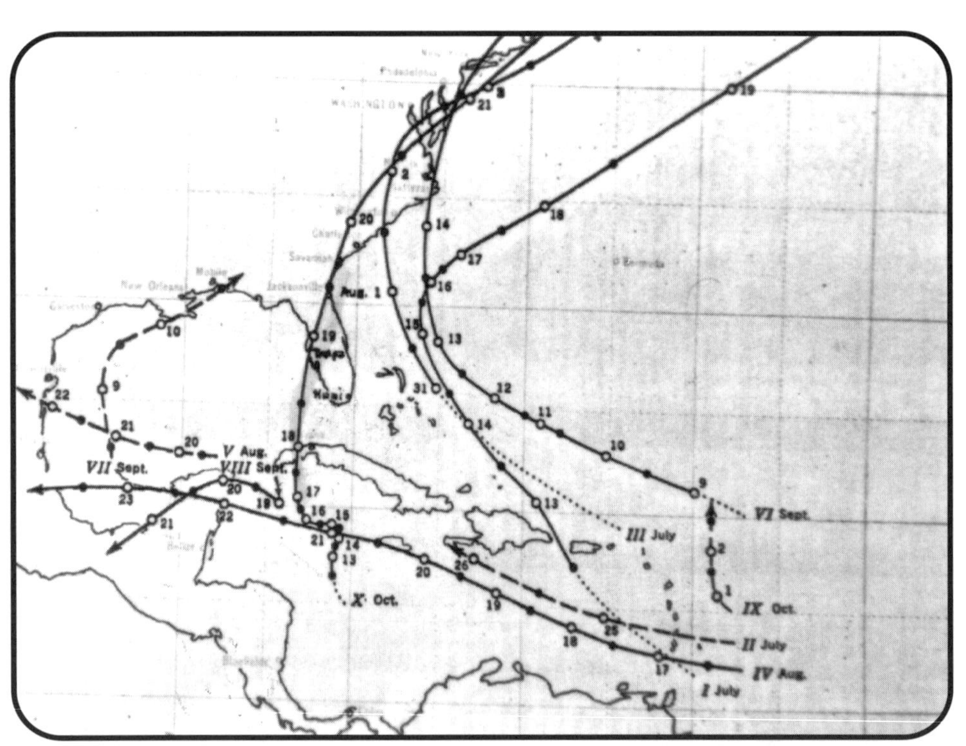

Photo: Hurricane Center, Miami

Hurricane map of 1944, illustrating the October storm that struck Venice

to airbases far inland, such as to Texas and Oklahoma. Where possible, troops were transferred to facilities that hopefully could withstand the force of the hurricane. All nonessential personnel were transferred to other bases or places where they would be safe from the storm. From Fort Myers north to Venice and Sarasota, all base personnel were housed in brick or concrete housing as protection from the winds. In Venice, the Kentucky Military Academy was used to house the base personnel.

Aircraft reconnaissance tracked the storm as it continued to move north. At 3:00 a.m. Eastern Standard Time on October 19th, the hurricane moved on shore at Nokomis, just north of Venice. Taking a course north-northeastward across Florida, the storm center skirted east of Tampa, over Dade City and Ocala, passing out to sea just south of Jacksonville.

Pvt. James Turston remembered the wind blowing so hard in Venice: *They had to put mattresses against the inside of the windows at the Kentucky Military Academy to prevent broken glass from blowing in and cutting everyone. We were packed in there like sardines. It seemed that the wind blew for hours, with bits of debris from palms and other plants flying everywhere. Every time something went flying through the air and struck the building it sounded just like a bomb going off. When the storm blew itself out they hustled us out of the building and sent us off to clean up the airbase. What a mess. Most of the tent frames and the few tents that were left up were destroyed. There was some damage to the hangar, if I recall correctly. We spent the following week just cleaning up the mess. Never did care for those blows!*

The hurricane was traveling at 20 mph and was classified as a severe hurricane. It had an unusually elongated eye, at times to 70 miles long. Winds of over 100 mph were experienced at Sanibel Light, Fort Myers and the Venice airbase. During passage of the hurricane over central Florida, gale force winds were experienced over the entire Florida Peninsula, as well as the coastal sections of Georgia.

At Key West all small craft were secured, and there was no loss of life. Near Fort Myers, damage from high tidal surges was most severe along the western Florida coastal area. Highest tides were reported from the Everglades north to Tampa, with heaviest losses reported along coastal Fort Myers. Winds lashed Sanibel and Fort Myers and sent water several feet over First Street causing severe damage, destroying piers in front of the Beach Hotel and the pier at San Carlos Boulevard. At Venice and Sarasota, airbases with vulnerable wooden structures and barracks were destroyed. Estimated damage in Florida to structures was set at $63 million. Crop damage to citrus and vegetables was set at an estimated $50 million. Military damages were relatively low due to the use of aircraft reconnaissance and the early warning system.

The first tropical storm of 1945 formed in the western Caribbean sea on June 20th. On the 23rd a reconnaissance plane flew into the storm about 120 miles off Apalachicola and estimated winds at 100 mph. Warnings alerted all base commanders. The storm diminished in intensity as it reached the west coast of Florida and passed inland between Brooksville and Dunnellon at about 4:00 a.m. on June 24th. The hurricane crossed Florida with exceptionally heavy rains and winds of 45 to 55 mph. About noon on June 24, 1945, the storm

Photo: Sarasota Historical Society

1944 hurricane that struck Venice and Sarasota airfields.

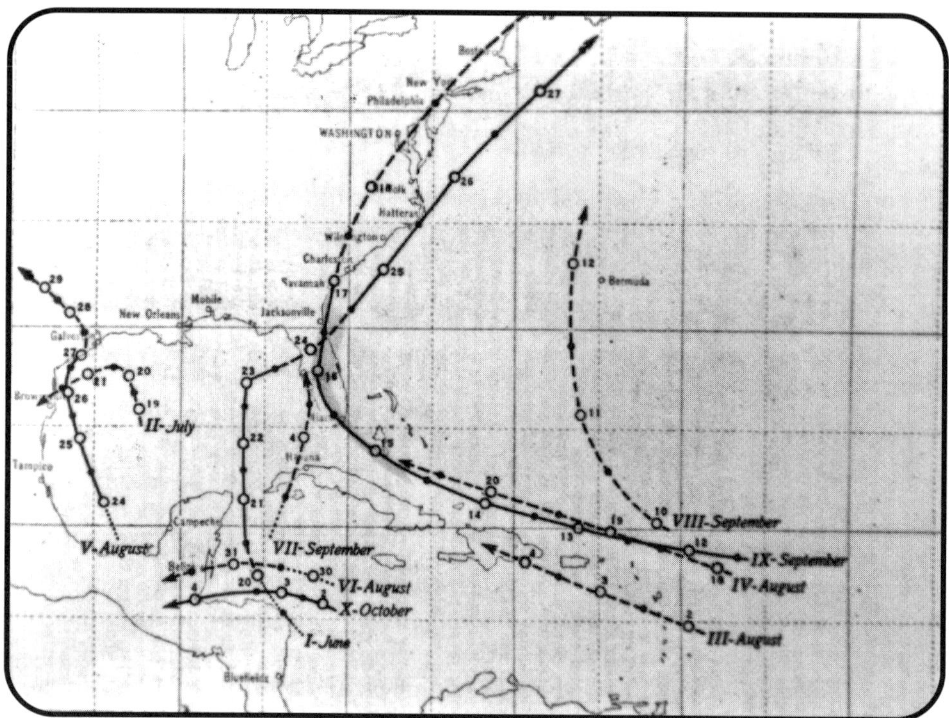

Photo: Hurricane Center, Miami

Hurricane track of 1945 with storm that struck NAS Richmond

moved into the vastness of the Atlantic, between Daytona Beach and St. Augustine.

Damage from the storm was not heavy and no deaths were reported. Tampa recorded 10.42 inches of rain within 24 hours, breaking all previous records for that area. In most areas passage of the storm was considered beneficial instead of damaging, as the heavy rains broke a 12-month drought.

First noted east of the Leeward Islands on September 11, 1945 a severe hurricane was about to strike Florida. It began a gradual curvature to the northwest while passing over the Great Bahama Bank during the night of September 14-15th. Severe hurricane warnings had been issued throughout Florida. All nonessential military personnel were evacuated to safe locations and once again all aircraft were flown to inland airfields.

When the hurricane alert was announced and it approached Miami, the Navy sent many of its aircraft to NAS Richmond. The huge wooden blimp hangars were considered adequate to shelter aircraft against the storm. Meanwhile, moving inland, the eye of the storm passed almost directly over the now-empty Homestead Army Air Force Base. Traveling northward toward Lake Okeechobee, the storm completely destroyed the town of LaBelle.

At NAS Richmond, the three huge wooden blimp hangars, each 1,060 ft. long, 300 ft. wide and over 180 ft. high, began to disintegrate under the 140 mph winds. Sparks created by the disintegration of the roof timbers ignited the stored high octane gasoline. Thousands of gallons of aviation fuel burned, producing temperatures in excess of 2,000 °F. Consumed in the triple inferno were 366 fighters, some private aircraft, 25 inflated and deflated

Photo: US Navy

Hurricane damage to dirigible hangars at NAS Richmond

Photo: US Navy

Aircraft damage as a result of being stored in dirigible hangar during 1945 hurricane

blimps, 150 automobiles and the Chief of the Fire Department office at the NAS Richmond base. Air operations were halted.

After destroying the towns of Perrine, Goulds, Princeton, Florida City, Homestead, Richmond, Redland and South Miami, the hurricane headed north into the rich fertile citrus farmland of central Florida. Lakeland re-corded winds to 80 mph by 7:30 a.m. eastern standard time. The highest velocity winds remained on the eastern side of the storm, developing 80 mph winds at Deland, Sanford and Melbourne. Winds of 75 mph were apparently maintained as the storm raced up the Florida Peninsula until the eye reached the Atlantic near St. Augustine at about 10 p.m. on the 16th.

Property damage to Florida from the storm was estimated to be $860 million of which $50 million was listed for Dade County alone. Four people died as a result of the storm, but the loss of life was kept to a minimum due to the early evacuation effected by the Red Cross.

Experiments with radar located at military installations throughout Florida and aircraft reconnaissance played valuable roles in the saving of lives and property. The lessons learned with aircraft being utilized in locating and tracking tropical disturbances were not forgotten. Today the role of the "Hurricane Hunter" aircraft has grown in importance and sophistication.

Chapter Fifteen
War Stories

The Bermuda Triangle

Even after World War II had come to an end, most air bases in Florida were operating at 100%. On December 5, 1945, five Navy TBM Avenger bombers disappeared on a routine training flight out of NAS Fort Lauderdale. The heavy single-engine bombers each had a pilot with a crew of a turret gunner and a radioman.

The big planes were to fly due east 123 miles, then 73 miles due north, past Grand Bahama Island to Great Sale Gay, then southwest 120 miles returning to Fort Lauderdale. This was considered a routine navigational flight. The flight commander was Lt. Charles Taylor, an experienced Navy aviator.

Lt. Robert Cox was flying near NAS Fort Lauderdale when he picked up a call on his radio from Lt. Taylor. Taylor reported his compasses were not functioning properly and therefore he assumed his flight was lost. Disorientation, which is not unusual to pilots, is made worse over water since there are few if any landmarks to navigate by.

Cox offered to fly northeast and try to guide Lt. Taylor using his radio. His request was denied by the flight officer with this remark, "Lost planes were routine, besides they always return." By this time weather over this part of the Atlantic was rapidly deteriorating, as a severe cold front with storm conditions was moving in.

When NAS Banana River was finally notified, they sent out two Martin Mariners. Twenty minutes after takeoff, one of the Mariners exploded, killing the crew. The remaining Martin was unable to locate the missing aircraft or crash debris.

For the next five days, all available naval ships and planes — Coast Guard, sub-chasers, the CAP and a British Air Search Squadron from the Bahamas — systematically searched the area for the missing aircraft. More than 200 available military aircraft from Fort Lauderdale, Fort Myers, Boca Raton, Miami, Sarasota, McDill, Orlando, Jacksonville, Banana River, Vero Beach and Key West joined in the largest peacetime search in history. Mainland Florida was searched by the military and thousands of volunteer civilians. Not a trace of the five TBMs was ever found.

The missing planes were all but forgotten until the early 1950s when magazine articles began to appear regarding missing ships and aircraft. Although many of these stories were either untrue or exaggerations, there remains the mystery of some of the "disappearances." The term *Bermuda Triangle* was coined in 1964 by Vincent Gaddiz in a story about the missing TBMs in *Argosy* magazine. Many news articles and books have been written about this truly Floridian adventure.

DOOLITTLE RAIDERS

Lt. Colonel Jimmy Doolittle and a select crew including a Navy Lieutenant landed a B-25 at Page Field at Fort Myers. Working for several days, the crew stripped down a B-25 Mitchell bomber to the barest of flying equipment. Anything that was not required to help the aircraft take off was removed.

Out onto the runway Doolittle and the Navy officer would go, pacing off a distance, recording information on some note pads, then going back to the hangar. These scenes occurred while the runways at Page Field were relatively short, before they were later extended. They would bring the bomber onto the runway, then revving the two engines until they sounded as though they would explode, Doolittle would roar down the airstrip. At a white line painted on the runway, he would pull the control wheel back into his lap. The bomber would seem to leap into the air, but it was always too far past the white line. It appeared strange to all the many onlookers. No one understood what they were attempting to accomplish nor why.

The purpose was to determine whether a B-25, loaded with bombs, could take off from an aircraft carrier's deck. If this could be accomplished, it would be possible to bomb Japan from a carrier at sea using B-25s. Once Doolittle proved it could be done, he went to train his selected crews at Eglin Army Air Force Base. It was not uncommon to see groups of B-25s flying just above the water along the west coast of Florida. After training in Florida, the famed Doolittle Raiders successfully bombed Tokyo.

Photo: Jean Cummings Collection

Ferry pilots and instructors at flight line

THE "CANNON BALL EXPRESS"

This was the title given to one of the strangest and longest military air routes used in World War II. Originating in Florida, aircraft of all types were flown to key airfields on the coast of Brazil, then after refueling and necessary light maintenance, on to the Gold Coast of West Africa. From the Gold Coast planes flew to other airfields in Africa. As the war in Africa was being won, some aircraft continued on to India. From India others flew on to China by way of the Himalayan Hump. Others departed India and flew to the East Indies, then on to the Philippines, Australia or islands of the Pacific war.

These transports and ferry planes, flown by both men and women, departed from Morrison Field at Miami, and from Homestead, Florida. Early in 1942 Pan American Airlines began hauling cargo to Karachi, India bound for Burma and China via the "Cannon Ball Express" route. The airline made 2,300 Atlantic crossings, logging more than 14,500,000 miles in one year! The now-defunct Eastern Airlines flew for the Atlantic Air Transport Command, logging some 33,480,000 miles, transporting 23,750 tons of cargo and 13,000 passengers. All Air Transport Command flights originated in Florida.

THE DIXIE DIVISION

The 31st Infantry Division originally consisted of National Guard troopers from Alabama, Louisiana, Mississippi and Florida. It was activated on November 25, 1940 and was commanded by Major General John C. Persons of Birmingham, Alabama. The Division reported to newly-built Camp Blanding. Basic training really did not begin until a lot of hard work by the troopers had cleared much of the tangle and morass of the scrub growth.

Returning from the Christmas holiday, the men started basic training as a unit with some the new inductees. The division was one of those early war units that participated in the famed Louisiana maneuvers.

Early in February 1942 the division was moved to Camp Bowie, Texas. From Camp Bowie the division went to Camp Pickett, West Virginia then to Camp Bradford where the troopers received amphibious training along the Maryland shoreline. On March 12, 1944 the 31st embarked from Hampton Roads, Virginia and after a very long time aboard rolling troop ships, arrived at Oro Bay, New Guinea on April 24, 1944.

The battle credits of the 31st include fighting in the steamy jungles of northern New Guinea, and on the islands of Morotai and Mindanao. Following the end of the war, the division remained on Mindanao until December of 1945 after which it was returned to the United States and was officially deactivated.

THE TOURISTS

Military contracts and war-related business may have alleviated most of Florida's economic depression, but there were many Floridians worried about tourism and the future after the war. Tourist attractions, such as horse and dog racing had been suspended, causing many gamblers and local businessmen to grumble. With the advent of gas rationing, transportation became a critical problem. With more and more troops being shipped overseas and the military bases providing more and better base housing, many hotels and inns suddenly found themselves without tenants. The hotel owners hurried to fill the vacancies with advertising campaigns designed to bring northern tourists to Florida.

The 1943-1944 winter season, even as the war raged on, soon produced increasing numbers of out-of-state license plates with motorists busily driving about the Sunshine State seeking fun and sun. The horse and dog tracks had re-opened along with the famed Orange Bowl (Louisiana State University played Texas A&M). Night spots and the casinos all thrived, much to the delight of local businessmen. Although strict Government regulations were still in effect, gasoline could be found easily (initially) on the black market, if you had the right money.

The rush to Florida during the winter of 1943-44 brought many of the usual millionaires and notables. Many found the conditions and prices most intolerable. The astronomical jump in the seasonable rates was prohibitive, especially for servicemen's families. Many sought shelter in tents, slept in cars and huddled in makeshift camps. The situation deteriorated when the tourists attempted to leave. Gas rationing restrictions had been tightened during the winter months leaving less gasoline available for the drive back north. In addition, due to increased troop movements, rail passenger space was limited. Tourists crowded rail stations with thousands seeking space. One estimate used by the railroads said it would take 2-3 months to get everyone north. The scene that followed seemed incredible. Tourists acted like war refugees, sleeping in railroad stations, in city parks, or wherever they could find shelter.

The Office of Defense Transportation solved the problem by allowing the Seaboard Railroad and the Florida East Coast Railroad to each add one extra train each day during the emergency. The first train left Miami loaded with 300 passengers, stopped at Jacksonville and picked up more coaches with 320 additional passengers, then headed north.

Newspapers poked fun at the "stranded refugees," blaming the tourists for their own greed. Harsh criticisms flashed between all levels of government and society, but as one wag commented, "Business is business is business."

COASTAL ARTILLERY

During World War II, the Army was given the responsibility for defending the continental United States. Confident that neither Japan nor Germany could mount an invasion of either coast, the military did little to prepare for such an eventuality. When Japanese submarines shelled a West Coast community and one shell scored a hit, coastal defenses, in addition to anti-submarine measures, were hurriedly developed. Field artillery battalion combat teams were stripped from various National Guard units and sent to strategic locations along the coasts. Heavy and light field artillery pieces were used to guard harbors and military beaches. Old Civil War harbor forts were once again used as emergency placements, until larger more permanent facilities could be assembled. As the war progressed, most of these artillery units were removed and sent overseas to combat areas.

Photo: US Air Force

Black airmen at squadron picnic, Dale Mabry Airfield

JIM CROW

Throughout Florida during the war years, black soldiers generally received substandard treatment and facilities. Long after service clubs, recreation halls, libraries and sports facilities were put in place for white servicemen, no such accommodations were in place for black soldiers. Melvin J. Bracken, Jr. remembers:

In those days Jim Crow was very much how the black man was kept in his place. Course we weren't called blacks back then, it usually was n-----s. I was stationed at Dale Mabry Army Air Corps Base at Tallahassee. Mostly I spent my time driving truck. Although I had a high school education, the Army did not think I was capable of being trained to do much more than drive a truck. You have to understand, anyone who had a high school education at the beginning of the war was in the real minority. My entire company was black except for the officers. The duty wasn't so bad, as long as you kept your nose clean. We didn't have much of any trouble with the white soldiers, at least at Dale Mabry as long as we did as we were told. The problem came in town. You see, we black soldiers had the idea that as long as we were in the Army and willing to die for our country, we should be treated like white soldiers. Not so!

Tallahassee was not a big city, as it is today, but despite the war, black soldiers were not allowed in downtown areas unless you were on duty. So we rode at the rear of the bus or on all-segregated buses. In town we had to spend our money in segregated areas, bars, hotels and restaurants. It was no different than before the war.

Fights were commonplace all over Tallahassee, with soldiers fighting each other or civilians. I was raised in New York, but I'd never seen so many folks spoiling for a fight. We supposed the people put up with us just so they could take our money, and that they did. The worse problem was for the black MPs. They kept them strictly segregated, patrolling black areas. When fights broke out, they would go crazy and nearly beat black soldiers to death. Everyone complained that the black MPs were harder on black soldiers, but no one did anything about it. Fights were so common, the brass finally restricted all troops to their own bases. The worse fights occurred when the crazy troopers from Camp Johnston arrived in town for a weekend pass. They would go wild. The worse was when blacks rioted in the black community called Frenchtown. Now you have to understand Frenchtown. It was the same as Harlem is to New York, and so all the black soldiers would go there. The fight turned into a race riot, with soldiers destroying just about everything in sight, and battling MPs and local police. It was something I shall never forget.

After the war, I went back to New York, worked my way through college on the G. I. bill, received a degree in education and spent the next 30 years teaching at the high school level, in a segregated school, of course. Retired, I now live near Jacksonville, Florida.

SECRET BASE

The military had long considered the use of various chemical weapons, especially the use of gases that would incapacitate large numbers of enemy troops in the battle area. With the development of chemical weapons, test sites located in remote areas were required. Several large production and test sites were established. When a tropical test area was needed, the U.S. Army looked to Florida and Panama for remote locations.

Northeast of Tampa, on present day Routte 301, was located the perfect site — Bushnell, a small town with a small population located in an area of open expanses. With a prevailing wind from the west, high humidity and even higher temperatures, it provided the Army with the ideal tropical testing area.

Very quietly the Army constructed the usual airfield with the usual size and the usual size barracks — lots of barracks listed as the U.S. ARMY FIELD PROJECT PROGRAM. Hundreds and eventually thousands of volunteer soldiers and sailors were sent to Bushnell as part of the Chemical Warfare Testing Program. The primary elements the volunteers were exposed to were the incapacitating gases. So well kept was the secret of the test site, few individuals outside of the test facility ever knew of the site.

ALLIED AIRMAN

I call it my term of sea duty, so states Jeremy Skillings of Toronto, Canada. *Like so many Allied airmen, many Canadians were sent to the United States for primary pilot training, and I was one of them. After our training at Lakeland, we were sent to Jacksonville for more training. From there we were scattered to different fields to train for different purposes. Six of us were sent in 1942 to Vero Beach for night fighter training. It was a Naval Air Station and we kept wondering why, as Royal Canadian Air Force troops we were trained by naval types. We flew F6F-5N Hellcats, specially rigged with a crude radar unit under the right wingtip.*

We flew in flights or four or five, with an experienced pilot. Mostly we flew just about every night over land to a preset destination, would I.D. it by radio and radar, then return to Vero Beach. Well, most of the planes returned to base. A whole lot never made it back. We kept the local CAP chaps busy searching the scrub for those who did not make it back. We never saw most of those that went down.

Me, well I took my turn and got really lost. I ended up over water with an engine that did not like me one bit! I successfully ditched that old crate in the Atlantic, which was no easy task, climbed into my little rubber boat and waited to be rescued, I prayed. I knew everyone would be looking for me, as someone had acknowledged my call for help. I don't think we were using the term "MAYDAY" then. Can't remember. Anyway, I bobbed about for three hours, and just after sun up, along came this two-master, a sailing ship. It had Coast Guard letters painted on it, so I knew it was ours. I felt just grand. They hauled me aboard, gave me some hot chocolate and let me go below to sleep, which I did with great relish. I was very happy to see those chaps.

I think I was asleep, maybe a half hour when I could hear all this shouting up on deck. Sticking my head out of the hatch, I could see that they were all excited about something. "What's up?" I asked one of the deckhands. "We're onto a U-boat!" he yelled, grinning from ear to ear. That's all we need, I can remember thinking at the time. I could not see any submarine.

I went on deck and watched everyone running around, pulling on ropes, getting some barrels set. 'What are those?' I asked. 'Depth Charges' I was told. I hoped they knew what they were about. We turned first one way then another, zigzagging all over the place. Then, all of a sudden, the boat straightened and some one yelled, "Over depth charges!"

One after the other, two depth charges went over the side. It seemed like forever before the two depth charges exploded, sending up huge fountains of water. But there was no hit, or perhaps no submarine. All my brain could think of was we had made the skipper of the submarine angry and that he would surface and sink us with his deck gun. But after searching for about an hour, the crew broke off and headed for port.

About half way to the beach a crash boat met us and took me off. So goes my only adventure at sea, and a good one it was. It was all of it, a great and exciting adventure, training in Florida. To me it was much as Churchill had stated about England. 'It was one large aircraft carrier.' Everywhere you went you met men and women in uniform, ships everywhere and aircraft of every type and kind filled the air. Those were indeed exciting days!

APPENDIX 1

FLORIDA MILITARY INSTALLATIONS, 1938-1945

ALLIANCE	AUXILIARY ARMY AIRFIELD, MARIANNA
ALTOONA	CIVIL AIRPORT/ AUXILIARY ARMY AIRFIELD
AMELIA CITY	BOMBING RANGE, NAS JACKSONVILLE
APALACHICOLA	ARMY AIRFIEILD
ARMOUR	CIVIL AIRPORT/AUXILIARY FIELD
AUBURN	OLF, NAS PENSACOLA
AVON PARK	BOMBING RANGE, ARMY
AVON MUNICIPAL	CONTRACT PILOT SCHOOL
BAGDAD	OLF, NAS PENSACOLA, NAS MILTON
BAKER	BOMBING RANGE, NAS JACKSONVILLE
BANANA RIVER	NAVAL AIR STATION O IN C COMMISSARY OPERATIONAL TRAINING UNIT VPB2 #3
BARIN	NAAS PENSACOLA
BASCOM	AUXILIARY ARMY AIRFIELD
BARTOW	ARMY AIRFIELD
BAUER	OLF, NAAS BRONSON
BAYOU	OLF, NAAS CORRY FIELD
BELL	OLF, NAAS CORRY FIELD
BELLE GLADE	AUXILIARY ARMY AIRFIELD/CIVIL AIRPORT
BELMORE	OLF, NAS JACKSONVILLE
BLACK CREEK	BOMBING RANGE, NAS JACKSONVILLE
BELL	BOMBING RANGE, NAS JACKSONVILLE
BOCA CHICA	NAAS ANTI-SUBMARINE WARFARE TRAINING UNIT
BOCA RATON	ARMY AIRFIELD

BOSTWICK	OLF, NAS JACKSONVILLE
BRANAN	OLF, NAS JACKSONVILLE
BRONSON	NAAS, NAS PENSACOLA
BROOKSVILLE	ARMY AIRFIELD
BROWNSVILLE	BRANCH INTELLIGENCE OFFICE, NAVY
BRUNSWICK (GA)	OLF, NAS JACKSONVILLE
BULOW	OLF, NAS DAYTONA BEACH
BUNNELL	OLF, NAS DAYTONA BEACH
BUSHNELL	ARMY AIRFIELD FIELD TRIAL PROJECT PROGRAM
CARLSTROM FIELD	ARCADIA, CONTRACT PILOT SCHOOL
CAMP BLANDING	ARMED FORCES INDUCTION STATION ARMY RECRUIT TRAINING PRIMARY FLORIDA P.O.W. CENTER
CAMPVILLE	OLF, NAS JACKSONVILLE
CANNON MILLS	AUXILIARY ARMY AIRFIELD, ORLANDO
CARLISLE	OLF, NAS JACKSONVILLE
CARRABELLE	AUXILIARY ARMY AIRFIELD, DALE MABRY CAMP GORDON JOHNSTON AMPHIBIOUS WARFARE TRAINING CENTER
CECIL FIELD	NAAS, NAS JACKSONVILLE BOMBER TRAINING CENTER
CEDAR KEYS	CIVIL AIRPORT/AUXILIARY ARMY AIRFIELD
CHAFFEE	BOMBING SITE, NAS JACKSONVILLE
CHOCTAW	OLF, NAAS WHITING FIELD
CLARCONA	BOMBING SITE, NAS JACKSONVILLE
CLEARWATER	CIVIL AIRPORT/AUXILIARY ARMY AIRPORT
CLEWISTON	ARMY AIRFIELD RIDDLE AIR SCHOOL P.O.W. CAMP SITE MUNICIPAL AIRPORT/AUXILIARY ARMY AIRFIELD CONNER FIELD/AUXILIARY ARMY AIRFIELD
CORAL GABLES	NAVY V-12 UNIT, UNIVERSITY OF MIAMI NAVIGATORS SCHOOL
CORRY FIELD	NAAS, NAS PENSACOLA
CRESCENT CITY	NAVAL AIR OPERATIONAL TRAINING COMMAND AUXILIARY BOAT FACILITY

CRESTVIEW	ARMY AIRFIELD, EGLIN #3
CROSS CITY	ARMY AIRFIELD SCHOOL OF APPLIED AIR TACTICS
CUMMER	OLF, NAS JACKSONVILLE
DAVIE	OLF, NAS MIAMI
DAYTONA BEACH	NAVAL AIR STATION AIR OPERATIONAL TRAINING BASE DAYTONA BEACH BOAT WORKS, INC.
DELAND	NAVAL AIR STATION AIR OPERATIONAL TRAINING BASE NAVAL MEDICAL REST CENTER (COLLEGE ARMS FLEET AIR DETACHMENT HOTEL)
DINNER KEY	U.S. NAVY AIR FACILITY
DORR FIELD	ARCADIA, CONTRACT PILOT SCHOOL
DUNEDIN	AMPHIBIAN TRACTOR DETACTMENT, USMC 7TH N.D.
DUNNELLON	ARMY AIRFIELD
EGLIN FIELD	ARMY AIR CORPS PROVING GROUNDS COMMAND HQ, lST PROVING GROUND TORPEDO SQUADRON (TEN AUXILIARY AIRFIELDS)
ELLIS	AUXILIARY ARMY AIRFIELD, MARIANNA
ELLYSON FIELD	NAAS, NAS PENSACOLA
FERNANDIA	OLF, NAS JACKSONVILLE
FLAGLER BEACH	CG BEACH PATROL STATION #5
FLEMING ISLAND	OLF, NAS JACKSONVILLE
FLOROSA	EGLIN #7 (VALPARISO)
FORMAN	OLF, NAS MIAMI
FRANCIS	OLF, NAS JACKSONVILLE
FT. LAUDERDALE	NAVAL AIR STATION SECTION BASE, INSHORE PATROL NAVAL AVIATION OPERATIONAL TRAINING BASE NAVAL ORDNANCE RESEARCH FACILITY BOAT FACILITY, PORT EVERGLADES DOOLEY'S BASIN AND DRYDOCK, INC. NAVAL MAGAZINES, PORT EVERGLADES NAVY ORDNANCE UNIT RADAR TRAINING SCHOOL (BEACH HOTEL) DIRECTOR OPERATORS SCHOOL FIRE CONTROL SCHOOL COAST GUARD PATROL BASE, PORT EVERGLADES

	ANTI-SUBMARINE AIR DETACHMENT
FORT MYERS	ARMY AIRFIELD, PAGE ARMY AIRFIELD, BUCKINGHAM FORT MYERS SHIPBUILDING CO. ARMY AIR FORCE FLEXIBLE GUNNERY SCHOOL FIGHTER TRAINING SCHOOLS, P-39, P-40, P-51
FORT PIERCE	NAVY AMPHIBIOUS TRAINING BASE RESCUE BOAT FACILITY UDT TRAINING BASE SCOUT AND RAIDER SCHOOL BEACH PARTY SCHOOL BRANCH INTELLIGENCE OFFICE ANTI-AIRCRAFT TRAINING CENTER ARMY CONBAT ENGINEERS SCHOOL OLF, NAS VERO BEACH
FT. WILLIAMS	HARBOR CONTROL POST
FOUNTAIN	AUXILIARY AIRFIELD, NAS PENSACOLA
FRANCIS	OLF, NAS JACKSONVILLE
GAINSVILLE	ALACHUA ARMY AIRFILED SCHOOL (UNIVERSITY OF FLORIDA) STENGEL AUXILIARY ARMY AIRFILED
GARNIERS	EGLIN #4
GONZALEO	OLF, NAS PENSACOLA
GREEN COVE SPRINGS	NAAS, NAS JACKSONVILLE
HALDER FIELD	AUXILIARY ARMY AIRFIELD, LAKELAND
HAMPTON FIELD	AUXILIARY ARMY AIRFIELD LAKELAND
HART FIELD	OLF, NAS JACKSONVILLE CIVIL AIRPORT
HERLONG	OLF, NAS JACKSONVILLE
HIALEAH	GIBBS HARRISON CO., INSPECTION STATION
HOBE SOUND	CAMP MURPHY, SIGNAL CORPS SCHOOL
HOEQUIST	AUXILIARY ARMY AIRFIELD, ORLANDO
HOLLEY	OLF, NAAS WHITING FIELD
HOLLYWOOD	NAVY RADAR SCHOOL, (HOLLYWOOD BEACH HOTEL) NAVAL TRAINING SCHOOLS NORTH PERRY FIELD, OLF TO MIAMI MACARTHUR FIELD, OLF TO MIAMI
HOLT	EGLIN #6
HOMESTEAD	ARMY AIRFIELD AIR TRANSPORT COMMAND

HORSESHOE POINT	AUXILIARY ARMY AIRFIELD, CROSS CITY
IMMOKALEE	AUXILIARY ARMY AIRFIELD, AVON PARK
JACKSONVILLE	NAVAL AIR STATION CHIEF, NAVAL AIR OPERATIONAL TRAINING STEVENS DRY DOCK AND REPAIR AVIATION SERVICE SCHOOLS NAVAL HOSPITAL OFFICE, DISTRICT INTELLIGENCE NAVAL COST INSPECTOR PORT DIRECTOR GIBBS GAS ENGINE CO. NAVAL AIR TRAINING BASES NAVAL AIR GUNNERS SCHOOL NAVAL AIR TECHNICAL TRAINING CENTER ARMED FORCES INDUCTION CENTER AIR BOMBERS SCHOOL AVIATION ENGINEERING OFFICERS SCHOOL NAVAL AIR SCHOOLS O IN C MARINE CORPS
JACKSONVILLE HEIGHTS	OLF, NAS JACKSONVILLE
JACKSONVILLE MUNICIPAL	ARMY AIRFIELD OLF, NAS JACKSONVILLE
JASPER	OLF, NAS JACKSONVILLE
JUPITER	NAVAL RADIO STATION NAVAL RADIO DIRECTION FINDER
KAY LARKIN	OLF, NAS JACKSONVILLE
KEYSTONE HEIGHTS	ARMY AIRFIELD
KEY WEST	NAVAL AIR STATION NAVAL OPERATING BASE REPAIR BASE NAVAL MAGAZINE CAPTAIN OF PORT NAVAL HOSPITAL ZONE INTELLIGENCE OFFICE BRANCH INTELLIGENCE OFFICE NAVAL RADIO STATION AUXILIARY AIR FACILITY, BOCA CHICA CONVOY CONTROL CENTER NAVAL FUEL ANNEX ANTI-SUBMARINE TRAINING UNIT, NAAS SUBMARINE BASE FLEET POST OFFICE COAST GUARD PATROL BASE MARINE BARRACKS FLEET SONAR SCHOOL

	MINE WARFARE OFFICE
KING	OLF, NAS PENSACOLA
KISSIMMEE	AUXILIARY ARMY AIRFIELD
LA BELLE	AUXILIARY ARMY AIRFIELD,CIVIL AIRPORT
LAKE BUTLER	OLF, NAS LAKE CITY
LAKE CITY	NAVAL AIR STATION AIR INSTRUCTORS SCHOOL
LAKELAND	ARMY AIR FIELD, DRANE FIELD AUXILIARY FIELD TO TAMPA LAKELAND MUNICIPAL FIELD, AUXILIARY ARMY AIRFIELD LODWICK AIR SCHOOL
LAKE WALES	AUXILIARY ARMY AIRFIELD/CIVIL AIRPORT
LAKE WORTH	AUXILIARY ARMY AIRFIELD/CIVIL AIRPORT
LANTANA	AUXILIARY ARMY AIRFIELD, PALM BEACH CAP HQ, FLORIDA
LEESBURG	ARMY AIRFIELD
LYNN HAVEN	NAVY PETROLEUM INSPECTORS OFFICE GENERAL AMERICAN TANK STORAGE AND TERMINAL CO.
LYONS	OLF, NAS PENSACOLA
MADISON	OLF, NAS JACKSONVILLE/CIVIL AIRPORT
MALABAR	OLF, NAS MELBOURNE
MALONE	AUXILIARY ARMY AIRFIELD, MARIANNA
MARATHON KEY	COAST GUARD PATROL BASE OLF, NAAS BOCA CHICA
MARIANNA	ARMY AIRFIELD ADVANCED STUDENT TRAINING
MASTER FIELD	OLF, NAS MIAMI
MAXWELL	OLF, NAS JACKSONVILLE
MAYPORT	NAAS, NAS JACKSONVILLE NAVAL AIR OPERATIONAL TRAINING COMMAND BOAT FACILITY
MELBOURNE	NAVAL AIR STATION AIR TRAINING FACILITY
MIAMI	NAS OPA-LOCKA CHAPMAN FIELD, ARMY CAPTAIN OF PORT COAST GUARD AIR STATION

	FREDERICK SNARE CORP. PRIGG BOAT WORKS DISTRICT INTELLIGENCE OFFICE DEGAUSSING STATION, CITY DOCK RECEIVING BARRACKS SUPPLY PIER, PIER THREE DESTROYER ESCORT TRAINING SCHOOL SUBCHASER SCHOOL, PIER TWO PAN AMERICAN AIRWAYS TRAINING SCHOOL ARMY INFORMATION CENTER OVERSEAS AIR CARGO TERMINAL LIAISON OFFICE, SOVIET NAVY COMMAND DISTRICT ORDNANCE OFFICE NAVAL TRAINING CENTER RADIO STATION NAVAL AIR GUNNERS SCHOOL REGIONAL AIR TRAFFIC COORDINATOR
MIAMI BEACH	HARBOR SIGNAL STATION NAVIGATIONAL TRAINING UNIT (NAS)
MIAMI SPRINGS	INSPECTOR, INTERCONTINENTAL AIRCRAFT INSPECTOR, CONSOLIDATED VULTEE CORP.
MIDDLEBURG	OLF, NAS JACKSONVILLE
MILE BRANCH	OLF, JACKSONVILLE
MILL COVE (DOCTOR'S ISLAND)	BOMBING RANGE, NAS JACKSONVILLE
MILTON	OLF, NAS PENSACOLA NAAS WHITING (NORTH AND SOUTH FIELDS)
MINNEOLA	AUXILIARY ARMY AIRFIELD
MONTICELLO	AUXILAIRY ARMY AIR FILED, MacDILL
MONTBROOK	AUXILIARY ARMY AIRFIELD
MORGAN CITY	NAVAL REPAIR FLOATING DRY DOCK
MOSSY HEAD	EGLIN #1
MYRTLE FIELD	AUXILIARY #3, CARLSTROM
NAPLES	AUXILIARY ARMY AIRFIELD, FT. MYERS NAVIGATORS SCHOOL ARMY GUNNERY RANGE
NAVARRE	OLF, NAS PENSACOLA
NEW SMYRNA	NAVY BRANCH INTELLIGENCE OFFICE NAVAL AIR OPERATIONAL TRAINING COMMAND BOAT FACILITY OLF, NAS DAYTONA BEACH
NICEVILLE	EGLIN #2

NO MANS LANDS ISLAND	NASSAU SOUND BOMBING SITE
NORTHEAST FIELD	AUXILIARY ARMY AIRFIELD, LAKELAND
NORTH POMPANO	OLF, NAS FT. LAUDERDALE
NORTHWEST FIELD	AUXLIARY ARMY AIRFIELD TO LAKELAND
OAKLAND PARK	OLF, NAS FT. LAUDERDALE
OCALA	AUXILIARY ARMY AIRFIELD, MacDILL GREENVILLE AVIATION SCHOOL
OKEECHOBEE	AUXILIARY ARMY FIELD, CONNERS
ORLANDO	AIR COMBAT CONTROL SQUADRON, ARMY AMPHIBIOUS #1 AIR COMBAT CONTROL SQUADRON ARMY AMPHIBIOUS #2 ARMY AIR FORCES SCHOOL OF APPLIED ACTICS
OSCELOA	OLF, NAS SANFORD
OSPREY	BOMBING RANGE, MacDILL
OUTLYING FIELD #4	OLF, NAS PENSACOLA
PACE	OLF, NAAS ELLYSON
PALATKA	AIR OPERATIONAL TRAINING BASE.
PALM BEACH	COAST GUARD TRAINING STATION TRAINING SCHOOL FOR USCG SPARS NAVAL CONVELESCENT HOSPITAL HQ CARIBBEAN DIVISION AIR TRANSPORT COMMAND
PANAMA CITY	PORT CAPTAIN BRANCH INTELLIGENCE OFFICE U.S. NAVY AMPHIBIOUS TRAINING BASE, ST. ANDREWS BAY
PAXON	OLF, NAS JACKSONVILLE
PENSACOLA	NAS CHEVALIER FIELD NAVAL HOSPITAL NAVAL TRAINING SCHOOLS AERIAL GUNNERY SCHOOL CELESTIAL NAVIGATION SCHOOL NAVAL AIR TRAINING COMMAND AVIATION GUNNERY INSTRUCTORS SCHOOL
PENSACOLA MUNICIPAL	OLF, NAAS WHITING FIELD
PERRY	ARMY AIRFIELD
PERRY NORTH/SOUTH	ARMY AIRFIELD, JACKSONVILLE
PINECASTLE	ARMY AIRFIELD

PINELLAS	ARMY AIRFIELD
PLANT CITY	AUXILIARY ARMY AIRFIELD to LAKELAND
POMONS	OLF, NAS JACKSONVILLE
POMPANO	OLF, NAS FT. LAUDERDALE
PORT EVERGLADES	NAVAL AIR OPERATIONAL TRAINING COMMAND BOAT FACILITY PORT DIRECTOR COAST GUARD BASE
PUNTA GORDA	ARMY AIR BASE B-17 TRAINING FACILITY
PUTNAM	OLF, NAS JACKSONVILLE
QUINCY	AUXILIARY ARMY AIRFIELD/CIVIL AIRPORT
RICHMOND	NAS(LTA) BLIMPS AIRSHIP HQ. SQUADRON DETACHMENT #21
RIDDLE FIELD	CLEWISTON- RAF TRAINING
ROSELAND	OLF, NAS VERO BEACH
RYAN	CIVIL AIRPORT-APOKA
ST. AUGUSTINE	COAST GUARD TRAINING STATION, FLAGLER COLLEGE ZONE INTELLIGENCE OFFICE CG BEACH PATROL STATION #3 OLF, NAS JACKSONVILLE
ST. MARYS	OLF, NAS JACKSONVILLE
ST. PETERSBURG	U.S. MARITIME SERVICE TRAINING STATION COAST GUARD AIR STATION,ALBERT WHITTED EGMONT KEY SIGNAL STATION JOINT ARMY/NAVY SEAPLANE REPAIR BASE PIPER-FULLER AIRPORT, OLF NAVY, USCG CRASH BOAT FACILITIES
SANFORD	NAVAL AIR STATION, TRAINING BASE
SANTA ROSA	OLF, NAAS WHITING FIELD
SARASOTA	ARMY AIRFIELD B-17 TRAINING FACILITY AUXILIARY ARMY AIRFIELD, MACDILL
SAUFLEY	NAAS, NAS PENSACOLA
SEBASTIAN	OLF, ROSELAND
SEBRING	ARMY AIR BASE, HENDRICK'S FIELD B-17 TRAINING BASE
SOUTH WEST FIELD	AUXILIARY #4, CARLSTROM

SPARKMAN FIELD	AUXILIARY #5, CARLSTROM
SPENCER	OLF, NAAS MILTON, NAS PENSACOLA
SPRUCE CREEK (SANSULA)	OLF, NAS DELAND
STUART	OLF, NAAS WITHAM, NAS VERO BEACH
STUMP	OLF, NAAS CORRY FIELD
SWITZERLAND	OLF, NAS JACKSONVILLE TRAINING FIELD
SMYRNA	NAVAL AIR OPERATIONAL TRAINING COMMAND BOAT FACILITY
TALLAHASSEE	DALE MABRY ARMY AIRFIELD NAVY BRANCH INTELLIGENCE OFFICE
TAMPA	DREW ARMY AIR BASE HILLSBOROUGH ARMY AIR BASE (SULFUR SPGS) PETER O. KNIGHT ARMY AUXILIARY FIELD MacDILL ARMY AIR BASE MULLET KEY GUNNERY RANGE TERRA CEIA GUNNERY RANGE TAMPA SHIPBUILDING CORP. (TASCO) ZONE INTELLIGENCE OFFICE PORT DIRECTOR NAVAL RECEIVING STATION SOVIET REPUBLIC, CHIEF OF MINE WARFARE NAVY RECRUITING STATION BUSHNELL-LYONS IRON WORKS HARBOR ENTRANCE SIGNAL STATION CIVIL WORKS DISTRICT
TARPON SPRINGS	NAVAL INTELLIGENCE OFFICE
TAYLOR FIELD	AUXILIARY ARMY AIRFIELD, OCALA
TELOGIA	POW CAMP
TENNILE	AUXILIARY ARMY AIRFIELD
TITUSVILLE	OLF, NAS SANFORD
TOMOKA	OLF, NAS DAYTONA BEACH
TROUT CREEK	OLF, NAS JACKSONVILLE
TYNDALL	ARMY AIR FORCE BASE GUNNERY RANGE GUNNERY TRAINING SCHOOL
VALKARIA	OLF, NAS MELBOURNE
VENICE	ARMY AIR BASE GUNNERY RANGE AIR MAINTENANCE TRAINING SCHOOLS POW CAMP

VERO BEACH	NAVAL SIR STATION AIR OPERATIONAL BASE
WACHULA	AUXILIARY ARMY AIRFIELD
WALLACE FIELD	CIVIL AIRPORT/AUXILIARY AIRFIELD
WELLS	AUXILIARY FIELD #3, CARLSTROM
WEST PALM BEACH	ARMY AIRFIELD, MORRISON FIELD AIR TRANSPORT COMMAND FACILITY
WEST PROSPECT	OLF, NAS FT. LAUDERDALE
WHITTING FIELD	NAAS, NAS PENSACOLA
WILLISTON	MONTBROOK AUXILIARY ARMY AIRFIELD
WITHAM	OLF, NAS VERO BEACH
WIMAUMA	AUXILIARY ARMY AIRFIELD
WITHACOOCHEE	AUXILIARY ARMY AIRFIELD
WINTER HAVEN	AUXILIARY ARMY AIRFIELD
"Y" FIELD	OLF, NAAS CORRY FIELD
YELLOW WATER	GUNNERY RANGE, NAS JACKSONVILLE
ZEPHYRHILLS	AUXILIARY ARMY AIRFIELD, MACDILL SCHOOL OF APPLIED AIR TACTICS

APPENDIX 2

ORAL HISTORIES

WALTER CZAJKOWSKI, JR.	WROCLAW, POLAND
MARGRET LOUISE DEVANEY	NOKOMIS, FL
ARTHUR E. SMITH	VENICE, FL
PERRY G. SNELL, JR	SARASOTA, FL
EX. GERMAN POW	NO NAME
JAMES THURSTON	OHIO/SARASOTA
MELVIN J. BRACKEN, Jr.	NEW YORK CITY
JEREMY SKILLINGS	TORONTO, CANADA
MARGARET PARRINELLO	LONGBOAT KEY, FL
BARBARA R. GRANA	VENICE, FL

APPENDIX 3

HISTORICAL RESEARCH ASSOCIATIONS

ARCADIA HISTORICAL SOCIETY
AVON PARK DEPOT MUSEUM
BOCA RATON HISTORICAL SOCIETY
BROOKSVILLE HERITAGE HISTORICAL SOCIETY
BARTOW HISTORICAL MUSEUM, POLK COUNTY
CHARLOTTE HARBOR AREA HISTORICAL SOCIETY
DAYTONA BEACH HISTORICAL SOCIETY
DELAND HISTORICAL SOCIETY
FLORIDA NATIONAL GUARD, CAMP BLANDING, HISTORIAN
FLORIDA STATE ARCHIVES
FORT LAUDERDALE HISTORICAL SOCIETY
FORT MYERS HISTORICAL MUSEUM
FORT PIERCE HISTORICAL SCOIETY
JACKSONVILLE NAS, STATION HISTORIAN
KEY WEST NAS, STATION HISTORIAN
MacDILL, BASE HISTORIAN
MAXWELL AFHRA, HISTORIAN
MELBOURNE HISTORICAL SOCIETY
PATRICK AFB, HISTORIAN
PENSACOLA NAS, STATION HISTORIAN
PINELLAS HERITAGE PARK AND HISTORICAL MUSEUM
POLK COUNTY HISTORICAL AND GENEALOGICAL LIBRARY
SARASOTA HISTORICAL SOCIETY
SARASOTA WACS ASSOC. CHAPTER #82
SEBRING HISTORICAL SOCIETY
ST. AUGUSTINE HISTORICAL SOCIETY
U.S. COAST GUARD HISTORIAN
VENICE HISTORICAL RESOURCE
VERO BEACH HISTORICAL SOCIETY

APPENDIX 4

RESEARCH REFERENCES

BISHOP, ELEANOR C.	*Prints in the Sand-USCG Beach Patrol WWII*, Pictorial Histories Publishing Co., Missoula, Montana
CARDWELL, SR. HAROLD D.	*History-Daytona Beach Naval Air Station 1942-1946*
COLES, DAVID J.	"Hell-By-The Sea," (Florida's Camp Gordon Johnston in WWII), *Florida Historical Quarterly*, VOL. LXXIII, NO. 1
COOPER, JR. RALPH W.	"The Genesis of Camp Blanding," (Brig. Gen. Ret.)
DEPT. OF COMMERCE	*Directory of Army/Navy Airfields December 1, 1944*
DUNN, HAMPTON	*Yesterday's Lakeland*
LIPPSTREUER, DOROTHY	*The Venice Advertiser*
NOAA	*NOAA Technical Memorandum NWS TPC-1 1966*, Paul J. Hebert, Jerry D. Jarrell, Max Mayfield "Monthly Weather Review, North Atlantic Hurricanes and Tropical Disturbances of 1945," H.C. Sumner
NOBLE,DENNIS L.	*The Beach Patrol and Corsair Fleet, U.S. Coast Guard*
PASCALE, PHILIP	Personal History, "My Stay at Venice Army Air Base," Venice Historical Resources
POLLARD, A.W. "SPIZZ"	*Hendricks Field, a Look Back.*
PRIOR, LEON O.	"Invasion of Florida," *Tropic, 1968*
SAPIO, VICTOR A. PhD	"Pensacola Naval Air Station, A Physical History"
SAWYER, MARTHA	"Lakeland," *The Lakeland Ledger*
SCHERR, ABRAHAM, PhD	"Presentation Paper, MacDill, 1994"
TEBEAU, CHARLTON W.	*A History of Florida,* University of Miami Press, 1971
WIDNER, ROBERT P.	Unpublished manuscript, *Aircraft Accidents in Florida from Pearl Harbor to the Atomic Bomb*, St. Petersburg
WYNNE, LEWIS H.	*Florida at War, 1993,* Saint Leo College Press

Other Wind Canyon Publishing Books

Aero Albums by Kenn Rust and Paul Matt — 20 volumes, each 48 pages and with 64 to 95 photos. Internationally acclaimed, republished after being out-of-print for 25 years. Wide variety of Pioneer, WWI, Golden Age, WWII and aviation history articles. Many 3-view drawings, profiles and illustrations.

Bonanza Around the World by Dennis Stewart — 1994 around-the-world air race by group of private pilots. Some were serious racers, others participated for the sheer adventure. Extraordinary journey where strange alliances developed and political expectations did not always turn out as planned.

Goodyear & Formula One Air Racing 1947-1967, Volume One by Robert Hirsch — Learn how this exciting sport caught on, the early players and governing organizations. This book tracks technological developments which allowed faster speeds and greater safety. 569 photographs, 88 scale drawings.

Goodyear & Formula One Air Racing 1967-1995, Volume Two by Robert Hirsch — Air racing had its ups and downs, but by 1967 it was firmly established as a sport here to stay. During this time, women pilots entered pylon racing, speeds continued to increase. 450 photographs, 74 scale drawings.

Crosswind by Patricia Valdata— A novel about a young woman's discovery of the unique and satisfying private world of soaring, as she rebounds from personal tragedy. A reader thinks about his/her own life, and the combination of choices and circumstances that put us where we are.

Just For the Love of Flying by Betty Rowell Beatty — About an incredibly modest and accomplished aviator, who at age 32 in 1954 traveled the length of Africa in an Auster Aiglet landing in 54 places during the 6-week flight. No radio, no ELT, no GPS. Just maps. Reminiscent of Beryl Markham.

The Legacy of the DC-3 by Henry Holden — The highly acclaimed comprehensive history of the people and events behind the DC-3/C-47, affectionately known as the *Gooney Bird*. Personal accounts of DC-3s flying themselves and hauling everything imaginable. 500 photographs and illustrations.

Upcountry Odyssey by Frank Bostwick — At age 68 the author biked solo from southern Florida to the Canadian border. A wonderful journey with tense moments, to be sure, but this story dispels myths about age-related limitations, and describes a country rich in human and natural resources and beauty.

The Wild Blue by Walter Boyne and Steven Thompson — Classic *New York Times* Best Sellers List novel about life in the Air Force and viewed to be the "book of record" on the opportunities, struggles and achievements available to those who love aviation and combine this love with an Air Force career.

A World Flight Over Russia by Brad Butler — In 1992 a group of private pilots circumnavigated the world in their small aircraft. This occurred at a moment in history when the Soviet empire had just unraveled, and the area was reeling from the shock waves. Spectacular b/w and color photographs.